Contents

Contents

The
SILENT BILLION SPEAK

by FRANK C. LAUBACH

FRIENDSHIP PRESS
New York

FRANK CHARLES LAUBACH has been a missionary to the Philippine Islands since 1915. He was born in Benton, Pennsylvania, and is a graduate of the Benton High School and Perkiomen Seminary. He received his A.B. at Princeton University and his Ph.D. from Columbia University. Upon his graduation from Union Theological Seminary in New York he became an ordained minister of the Congregational Church.

When first sent to the Philippines by the American Board of Commissioners for Foreign Missions, Dr. Laubach was assigned to general missionary work in Mindanao. Thus there were laid at once the foundations of his friendship with the Moro people, and among them he has since lived except for a term of service on the faculty of Union Theological Seminary in Manila.

At his station in Dansalan on Lake Lanao in northern Mindanao, Dr. Laubach founded in 1930 the Maranaw Folk Schools, and, as a part of his mission of interpreting Christianity among the half million Moslems under the American flag, began to reduce their language to a simple form of writing and to teach adults to read. The story of a world-wide campaign against illiteracy, which grew from that beginning, is the story unfolded in this book.

Dr. Laubach was in the United States on furlough when the Philippines were occupied by the Japanese in 1942, and in the interval he has been cooperating with both private and public agencies in the effort to extend literacy among adults in Mexico, the West Indies, and Central and South America.

This book has been manufactured in compliance with orders of the War Production Board for conserving paper and other materials

Foreword

IN THE summer of 1941 I spent a fortnight in Hawaii waiting for the Clipper to take me to the Philippines. The single experience that helped me more than any other to prepare for the long world journey ahead of me came through a morning's conversation with Frank Laubach on the veranda of a little cottage outside of Honolulu where he happened to be staying for a short time. This remarkable spiritual leader opened his heart and mind to me concerning his faith and purpose and vision. It was here that I came to see the plan for world literacy, not as a detached project or a fantastic dream, but as a practical statesman-like venture motivated by a consuming passion for the Truth that would make men free.

Frank Laubach will tell you his story in these pages. It is a tale of adventure, a demonstration of endurance, and a testament of faith. It contains the key to a new world order. This is not too strong a statement, for the world conflict is basically a war of ideas. How can men learn without a teacher? How can they think if, seeing, they do not understand? If the struggle of today is to free the oppressed millions, of what value is it to liberate their bodies and not release their minds? A Christian victory and a righteous and durable peace will come only as the mind and soul of a weary and broken world are fed upon "whatsoever things are true, whatsoever things are honest, whatsoever things are just, whatsoever things are pure, whatsoever things are lovely, whatsoever things are of good report."

The Foreign Missions Conference of North America, in which one hundred twenty-one boards and societies of the United States and Canada cooperate in the world Christian mission, counts the goal of world literacy and the influence of Christian literature a major task, an unlimited opportunity, and a tremendous and far-reaching force for the building of the kingdom of God. Frank Laubach is a special counselor and representative in this united effort. Following his pioneering achievements and fruitful cooperation with other devoted workers striving for the eradication of illiteracy and the creation of Christian literature in the Philippines, India, and Africa, Dr. Laubach was sent late in 1942 to spend six months campaigning for these causes in a number of the Latin American republics. As this prophet of Christian enlightenment again travels up and down our continent, may this book prepare the way for him, undergird him, and remain to keep the fire of Truth burning after he has passed by.

Charles Tudor Leber
Chairman, Committee on World Literacy and Christian Literature of the Foreign Missions Conference of North America

New York City
May, 1943

CHAPTER ONE

After the Silence of the Centuries

THREE out of five of the human race cannot read nor write—this was the startling revelation made in 1927 by James F. Abel, of the United States Bureau of Education. In Asia and Africa alone over a billion people are illiterate, nine persons out of every ten—half the human race. This cold type cannot tell you what that means. You think it is a pity they cannot read, but the real tragedy is that they have no voice in public affairs, they never vote, they are never represented in any conference, they are the silent victims, the forgotten men, driven like animals, mutely submitting in every age before and since the pyramids were built. It is a human weakness not to become aware of suffering unless we hear a cry. The illiterate majority of the human race does not know how to make its cry reach us, and we never dream how these millions suffer.

The most bruised people on this planet, the naked, the hungry, the fallen among thieves, the sick, the imprisoned in mind and soul, are the twelve hundred million illiterates, three-fifths of the human race. At least a billion are virtual slaves. Take India for illustration. She had over three hundred and forty millions of illiterates at the time the 1941 census was taken, 88 per cent of her people; and almost every illiterate is in debt all his life—and his children and his children's children after him. He does not know how much his debt is nor whether the interest is correct. The money-lender takes all he can take and still keep his victim alive—for it would be silly to kill the animal that makes him rich! In one form or another this is the black sorrow of nearly every illiterate in the world. More than half the human race is hungry, driven, diseased, afraid of educated men in this world and of demons in the next.

I have not only seen these people across Asia and Africa, but have sat beside many of them and taught them one by one, and have seen a new light kindle in their eyes; love and hope began to dawn as they stepped out of blindness and began to read. I know that we could free this multitude from their tragic bondage; indeed, their emancipation has already begun.

The curve of literacy, which has been nearly stationary in Asia and Africa and Russia for centuries, has turned upward recently, especially in the past twenty years. A hundred million more adults read today than twenty years ago. If that curve follows its present trend, within fifty years we shall have five hundred million new readers stepping out of the silent ranks of illiteracy to speak for the first time. This is not only exciting news. It is the most stupendous, the most arresting, and it may be the most ominous fact on this planet. Nothing can stop it now.

It will be wonderful or terrifying, depending upon whether these vast multitudes awaken with their hearts full of Christ's love or with their hearts full of hate. They will bless or blast the world. That is why the church must step to the front and take a leading share in the mighty upsurge of the sunken half.

We must not only help them rise but we must also put reading in their hands, the right kind of reading; and that is a staggering task. The literacy campaigns now under way are going to double the world's readers! In China and India, where through recent decades more than nine-tenths of the people have been illiterate, a mighty tide is now rising. Eight hundred millions in those countries alone will be reading before we are ready. Ninety-five out of a hundred Africans are still illiterate. But campaigns are starting all over that continent. Africa will be reading—before we are ready. A billion people now illiterate will be reaching out with hungry minds for something to read. Will they be fed with the message of Christ or with atheism? Will they read love or hate? Whatsoever is sown in their minds, the world will reap. And what will happen when these hundreds of millions shall speak "after the silence of the centuries"?

For ages Asia and Africa, with three hundred million more people than all the rest of the world together, have been sunk in apathy and stagnation. They followed in the footsteps of their ancestors, ignoring the rest of the world.

They believed it was wrong to break with any of the customs of the past. But with our imperialism, our business invasions, our missions, our radios, our airplanes, we have stabbed these peoples awake, and now the passion for progress burns like fire in their veins. They make more changes now in ten years than they used to make in a thousand years.

But as Asia and Africa attacked their enormous handicap of illiteracy they were confronted with a surprising difficulty. Modern medical science has been more successful than education. We helped them stamp out smallpox, cholera, bubonic plague, malaria, typhus, and other diseases that had kept their populations stationary, and now their populations are multiplying with ever increasing rapidity, faster than they can be educated. In India, between the 1921 and 1931 censuses, the number of literate persons increased by five millions, but the population increased by the staggering total of thirty-three millions, six times as fast as they could be taught to read.

This inability to catch up with their rising populations is making governments desperate. They eagerly welcome any suggestions that promise relief. It is here more than at any other point that they feel the need of missionary help. In India in 1939 every state, province, and presidency followed the lead of missions in establishing literacy campaigns. Those of us traveling over India in this cause found maharajahs, prime ministers of Indian states, college presidents, governors, Mr. Gandhi, Mr. Nehru, important leaders of all communities—Hindu and Moslem as well as

Christian—giving this movement their personal support and many of them attending literacy conferences conducted by missionaries. The leaders of Africa were equally cooperative. It was the same in China. Here is a cause in which every country believes. If the Christian church will help these countries out of their dilemma, it will win their cooperation and their hearts. I know many missionaries who are permitted to teach illiterates in prisons and other places that have been closed to them for any other purpose.

Teaching illiterates is proving to be a wonderful way to bring people to Christ. If you sit down beside an illiterate as your equal, your heart overflowing with love for him, and with a prayer on your lips that you may help him to a new vision; if you never frown nor criticize, but look pleased and surprised, and praise him for his progress, a thousand silver threads wind about his heart and yours. You are the first educated man who ever looked at him except to swindle him, and he will be so mystified by your unusual kindness that he is likely to stop and ask: "How do you expect to get paid for this? I have no money." Then you have your chance to say:

"I do not want any pay. I have learned this from Jesus. He spent all his time helping people free of charge. From the moment he awoke in the morning until he closed his eyes at night, he was looking around asking whom he could teach, or heal, or encourage, or defend, or save. I think that is a beautiful way to live. If we were all like Jesus, this world would be a paradise. So I thought I would try helping people just because I love them. And I have discovered the secret of happiness! When I am teaching you it makes my heart sing. When I have finished teaching you, I want you to go and teach your neighbors. Don't take any money for it, and your heart will sing! Brother, we have found the secret of happiness."

He goes out and teaches others, his heart sings, and he learns to love Jesus. The only irresistible gospel is love in action—helping people where they are in desperate need. If we serve the illiterates and then tell them the gospel after we have won their hearts, they will believe in Christ because they believe in us.

Teaching illiterates is a means of extending the gospel, moreover, because every Christian needs to read his Bible. Wherever a church contains many illiterates, it feels weak and unhappy until it has taught them to read. It finds that illiterates just emerging from non-Christian habits need constant personal attention to keep them from sinking back into the old life. They could gain new power to overcome if they could read the Gospels, and hymns, and Sunday school journals, and prayer books. Moreover, illiterates have no influence with the educated people among whom they live. For these and other reasons it is universally recognized that literacy is a first objective in every Protestant mass movement.

LITERACY FOR EVERYBODY A NEW IDEA

The belief that everybody has a right to read and write is modern; it came out of the Protestant Reformation. In ancient and medieval times, perhaps one in twenty, perhaps one in a thousand, could read. It varied in different countries. When the leaders of the Protestant Reformation taught their followers to search the Scriptures instead of consulting a priest, reading became a practical necessity for anybody who tried to be a first-rate Christian. Johannes Gutenberg met an acute need in 1450 when he invented moveable type, and thereafter every well-to-do home could afford to have a family Bible instead of only one Bible for a town or province. Then Luther, Tyndale, and other heroes flew in the face of orthodoxy by actually translating the Bible from sacred Latin into vulgar German and English so that people could learn to read it without learning Latin. Then came democracy with its radical teaching that everybody had a divine right to rule and therefore to have a little education. So democracy, Protestantism, and literacy are triplets. The first Sunday schools in England were established to teach people how to read the Bible and to do easy numbers. In Wales the Sunday school still teaches reading, writing, and 'rithmetic.

In the United States our literacy picture is still spotty. In various parts of the country illiteracy ranges from a low of 1.4 per cent to a high of 9.6 per cent of the population over ten years of age; and among certain racial groups in some sections as many as 22 per cent are still unable to read. In 1900 the illiteracy for our whole country was 10.7 per cent. Vigorous campaigns by government and private teachers reduced this to 4.3 per cent by 1930. Estimates for 1941 further lower it to 3 per cent. This is still higher than the Netherlands, Germany, Denmark,

Norway, Sweden, and Switzerland, all of which claim less than 1 per cent of illiteracy. These countries had a simpler problem than ours, however. They can teach reading in half the time it takes us, because their alphabets are regular and phonetic, while our English alphabet is "confusion worse confounded."

Japan also has better literacy statistics than ours. She claims that her illiteracy is below one per cent. Nobody knows the genius who invented the Japanese *kana* syllabary a thousand years ago. There is a symbol for every syllable and these are arranged in perfectly logical sequence so they are easy to memorize. *Kana* was already waiting to make literacy easy when Admiral Perry opened Japan to the West in 1853. Japan soon started to take mighty strides in progress and education. Every registered child was compelled to go to school. The fact that everybody reads books and newspapers is one of the secrets of her power. No other country in Asia is over twenty per cent literate, while most of them are less than ten per cent.

WHAT JIMMY YEN DID FOR CHINA

The Chinese did not, until recent years, have an alphabet of their own. Their characters represented ideas instead of sounds, while our Roman letters represent sounds and not ideas. The Chinese talk in monosyllables, which not only saves their breath but gives them a language simple in the extreme. They have twenty-four consonant sounds to start off or end their words and sixteen vowel and diphthong sounds to use with consonants. Because of their use of monosyllables and the fact that some letters are never found except at the beginning while others are found only at the end of the words, they can have only about five hundred words so far as sound is concerned. Fortunately, by using a variety of tones or inflections, they multiply this number to well over two thousand. Nevertheless, each word often has from ten to twenty possible meanings. Laugh at them if you will, only remember that we have some of these same troubles with our Anglo-Saxon monosyllables. For example, to ("to" has at least ten meanings) two, too; or do, due, dew; or u, you, ewe; or hew, hue, whew! We indicate different meanings by very bad spelling. When Chinese talk, they show what they mean by tones, and glides, and looks, and gestures. Obviously they cannot very well write tones and gestures with an alphabet. So they have shorthand pictures called ideographs—separate characters for every meaning of every word. A few years ago the Chinese did adopt an alphabet; it is useful to help illiterates to pronounce, but, as in Japanese, the characters have to be printed beside the spelled words to show what they mean. There is a New Testament in Mandarin with the words spelled down the left column and the characters beside them down the right column.

In spite of these difficulties of language, China, in the past quarter-century, has been the scene of one of the world's outstanding movements for literacy. It will always be associated with the name of Dr. James Yen, a Yale graduate—one of those brilliant Chinese who absorb all American has and take it back to China for the good of their people. In 1914, during the first World War, he was called to Europe by the Young Men's Christian Associa-

tion to work for the two hundred thousand Chinese la-
borers building trenches in France. "Jimmy" Yen started
a paper for them, the *Laborer's Weekly,* confining his
articles as far as possible to the thousand most commonly
used Chinese characters. These thousand characters he
arranged in four books, each book containing twenty-five
lessons, with ten characters in each lesson. By learning
ten characters a day, the student could master two hundred
and forty characters in one month or all the thousand
characters in four months. These lessons were so popular
that the coolies began to think themselves lucky to have
been brought to France.

When the war was over, Dr. Yen returned to China,
where he found the illiterates in every province eager to
learn his thousand characters.

One of the fine things about his literacy program in
China was that at least nine different kinds of experiments were undertaken in different provinces at the same
time, so that the results might be compared—how many
were taught in a year, how much it cost for each pupil,
how many enrolled, how many kept coming, and how long
it took them to learn.

In Hunan Province, in 1922, Dr. Yen and the group of
young experts whom he had enlisted in his cause began
the campaign by trying to create what they called a
"climate of willingness to go to school." They printed
fifteen hundred posters picturing how China is hindered
by ignorance. They distributed thousands of handbills
urging education. The governor put up on hundreds of

street corners proclamations that the people must learn
to read. A law was passed that every illiterate should be
taxed until he had learned one thousand characters and
could pass the examination. There were meetings of shop-
masters. There was a general parade by college and middle
school students bearing banners saying, "An Illiterate Is
a Blind Man," "Is Your Son Blind?" "Can You Stand It
to See Three-Fourths of China Blind?" They had huge
mass meetings. Eighty teachers were recruited from the
government and from mission schools; all they received
was four dollars a month for transportation. Then seventy-
five teams set out to visit shops, homes, and streets, and in
three afternoons fourteen hundred persons volunteered to
study—ricksha pullers, beggars, scavengers, fuel gatherers,
pig buyers, and peddlers. Classes were opened in sixty
places, sometimes two classes under one roof. Of the
original number, twelve hundred stayed through, and
nine hundred and sixty-seven passed the examinations.

Shansi Province, using equally original methods, raised
its literacy by ten per cent in ten years, and several other
provinces claim to have done as well. It is estimated that
since 1926, ten million persons have learned the twelve
hundred characters considered necessary for simple reading. The average cost for all China was $1.40 per pupil.

The invasion of China by Japan in 1937 did not stop
this mass education, but rather stimulated it. The whole
program was taken over by what is called the People's
Military Training Corps. In the city of Kweilin the boys
and girls of middle schools taught their elders while they

were crowded into caves near the city during airplane bombardments. It helped keep their minds off their worries. Now they say that, thanks to the Japanese bombs, illiteracy has been wiped out of the city.

WHAT RUSSIA HAS DONE IN TWENTY YEARS

Far and away the largest literacy campaign carried on in all history has been that of Russia since 1921—though China and India together will teach seven times as many before their compaigns are finished! Russia under the czars was far behind other European nations in literacy. In 1920 her literacy was given as 31.9 per cent in government reports, but less than 9 per cent really were able to read intelligently, as they now confess. This illiteracy ran directly across Lenin's idea of government by the masses. On every occasion he placed literacy among the first necessities for a communist government. "An illiterate people cannot build a communist state," he said. "An illiterate person is outside the sphere of politics. The first thing he needs is to be taught the alphabet!"

In a dictatorship, things can be accomplished swiftly by government orders. Lenin began by ordering all spelling changed. Russian spelling had been as bad as ours is in English. A perfectly phonetic alphabet was adopted in place of the old one. The second change Lenin made was to teach the languages that people spoke. The old czarist government had refused to teach any but the official Russian language. Lenin saw that Russia would not be literate in a hundred years if he tried to teach only one language, for there are fifty-eight important languages in the U. S. S. R. (two hundred and eighty-two if all sub-dialects are counted). Some of the Russian languages had used Arabic script, but many had never been written at all—they were only spoken. The Communists reduced these fifty-eight principal languages to writing, using the new alphabet, and prepared textbooks in them. In 1922 they made education free for everybody, irrespective of race or color. Children were put into vocational schools and every child was taught to read and to do something useful with his hands.

Adults, both men and women, were also taught to read in Russia-wide campaigns. Two and a half million "cultural soldiers" were recruited to teach without pay, and these were commanded by hundreds of thousands of special paid teachers. School children were organized into "Down with Illiteracy Societies," which surveyed their towns to find out how many illiterate adults there were. After August, 1931, illiteracy became a legal offense!

The campaign gathered momentum with astonishing speed: in 1927, 1,300,000 persons were taught; in 1928, 2,700,000; in 1929, 10,500,000; and in 1930 the number more than doubled—22,000,000 persons were officially recorded as having learned to read. In 1933 Stalin announced that ninety per cent of the U. S. S. R. could read and write. There were several tribes that began with a literacy level as low as eight-tenths of one per cent and that became wholly literate. A nation of one hundred and sixty million people had been made literate in fifteen years!

UNIVERSAL LITERACY: CURSE OR BLESSING?

As Dr. John R. Mott once declared, "The alphabet is the most dangerous weapon ever put in human hands." It is like science—it may bless the world or destroy it. It is like science in another respect—nobody can stop either science or literacy now: all we can do is to guide them. This is why people with the ideals of Christ must take a leading part in teaching illiterates and in producing literature.

I had an interesting conversation with Mahatma Gandhi in 1935 when I first visited India. We had just completed a reading chart in the Marathi language and I took it to Wardha to show Gandhiji what we were attempting. He was sitting on the floor. I sat down cross-legged in front of him and unrolled the Marathi chart. He glanced at it, then looked up, and, to my amazement, said:

"I doubt whether India ought to become literate."

"You are the first person I ever heard say that," I said, hardly believing my ears. "What do you mean?"

"The literature you publish in the West is not fit for India to read. Look at what you are writing and selling us on any railway stand." He was right about that—I had looked! Without waiting for my reply, this man, revered as a saint by millions, gave me a second punch before I had recovered from the first—and don't you agree that this was "the most unkindest cut of all" to a Christian missionary?

"Many of the greatest benefactors of the human race have been illiterate—Mohammed, for example." My answers, I think, came out of heaven. At least I haven't been able to think of any others as good in seven years.

"Mr. Gandhi," I said, "you are right. But on the other hand, millions of us admire you and have read your books with great blessing. If you had not written these books and if we had not learned to read, we should never have heard of you."

Mr. Gandhi dropped his head and said meekly, "I think I would have done a little good."

The other answer came to me that instant and I let him have it: "The greatest single blessing that ever came to this world was the life and teaching of Jesus Christ. If Christ's life had not been written and if we had not been able to read the Gospels, we would know very little about him."

Mr. Gandhi shook his head up and down slowly and silently for a few moments, and he looked through me every time his head came up. I wish I knew what he meant by that head shake. He changed the subject.

"I really do believe in literacy for India," he said at last. "Indeed, I have probably been instrumental in teaching thirty thousand indirectly myself. But by far the largest question for India is how to feed her hungry multitudes."

"This," I said, "is exactly why India needs to become literate. The right way to lift the masses above hunger is to teach them to lift themselves. Your illiterates have been the victims of educated scoundrels who have kept them in debt all their lives. Literacy is the only road I see to their complete emancipation."

The truth is that Mr. Gandhi, like nearly all Indian leaders in those years, was in despair about teaching people so underfed and so overworked as the masses of India are, and believed that economic relief had to come before they could take even the first step toward education. But in subsequent years, first in one corner of India, then in another, ever larger literacy movements began to appear, indicating that perhaps, after all, literacy is the horse that should come before the cart. In more recent years Mr. Gandhi has become more and more emphatic in saying that illiteracy can be and must be wiped out in India. In 1939 he wrote in the papers: "I am converted, and now believe that literacy should be required for the franchise. If each one of us will teach one illiterate, we can make India literate in no time!"

And now all India is on the march to become literate!

But before I tell that story, I shall first go back to 1929, when a new approach to adult literacy was developed under the American flag among the Moros of Mindanao in the Philippines, and then I shall trace the spread of that "Philippine method" over the world. I came from these experiences with my faith unwavering in the very face of this mad war, because I have seen how easy it is to win the love of peoples of any race when we really love and serve them unselfishly.

CHAPTER TWO

A Literacy Campaign from the Inside

THE literacy campaign that began among the Moros of Lanao Province of Mindanao in 1930 has attracted some attention in the United States, but much more in Asia, Africa, and Latin America. This chapter is an intimate tale of that campaign; why it started, how it felt as we carried it on, and what it did to the Moros. During those years I wrote weekly letters to my father, and in this book I have quoted frequently from them.

When Effa Seely and I were married in 1912, we chose as our field for foreign service the great island of Mindanao in the southern Philippines. It appealed both to our religion and to our patriotism. We had first become interested in this island when Effa's cousin, Harry Edwards, and another fellow-townsman, Joe Albertson, went there as teachers in 1901, among the first six hundred teachers sent to the Philippines by our government on the famous transport *Thomas*. Harry and Joe wrote back vivid accounts of the Moros of Mindanao and Sulu, the worst trouble-makers American soldiers had ever faced.

In 1915, just before we left for Mindanao, there was a farewell meeting at the Harvard Church in Brookline, Massachusetts, and several of us departing missionaries gave five-minute speeches. I remember as though it were yesterday what I said, for I had reached my decision only after a struggle with selfish ambition:

"If I were in a battle and with no orders from my captain, I would be a coward if I fought where we were winning; I would be a man if I fought where our ranks were thin and we were losing the battle. We *are* in a battle for Jesus Christ, to conquer the world, and the ranks are thinnest and the battle hottest in the Orient. So we are going where we are needed most."

When we reached Mindanao that year we found its mountains and lakes as beautiful as we had expected. We visited lovely blue Lake Lanao, which lay in the crater of an ancient volcano half a mile above sea level, with a raging river plunging twenty miles to the ocean. But the atmosphere of the place was tense. The government was having continuous trouble with the Moros.

Army officers whom we met on arriving told us that an inexperienced missionary talking religion to the Moros would only make matters worse and they did not think the Moros would be ready to hear us for several years. So we moved on and settled at Cagayan, a hundred miles away, where conditions were more favorable, but returned to Lanao a month every summer to enjoy the cool air and to watch for the time when work could begin with the Moros.

The Moros, in point of fact, had been fighting and hating Christians ever since Magellan discovered the Philippines in 1521. It happened that just twenty-nine years before that date, in the famous year 1492, back in Spain, the Moors (or Moros as they are called in Spanish) had been hurled across the Strait of Gibraltar into Morocco. When the Spaniards went down around South America, crossed the Pacific Ocean, and ran into Mindanao in the southern Philippines, they found people practising the Moslem religion, and so made the big mistake of calling them "Moros," just as Columbus had made the mistake of calling American natives "Indians."

But the Spaniards made the far worse mistake of waging war on these Filipino "Moros" just because they had been fighting the African Moros. What consummate stupidity! They gave them the wrong name, then said, "Now you are Moros, too, so we will fight you!" It was almost the silliest war on record. In three hundred and seventy-seven years the Spanish troops never conquered the Moros of Mindanao. When the United States took the Philippines in 1898, the Moros resisted the new rulers as fiercely as they had resisted the Spaniards. General Pershing became famous fighting these Lanao Moros. Not until 1917 did the American troops regard the situation sufficiently under control to permit them to move out of Lanao and leave in the hands of Filipino soldiers the camp that Pershing had built.

It was not until 1929 that the time seemed ripe to open the Lanao station. Leaving my wife and my son Bob in a school north of Manila, I went to Lanao alone. My colleagues, the Reverend and Mrs. Frank J. Woodward, who had reached Mindanao a year after our arrival and who were working along the coast of that island, had built a little summer cottage close to the military camp. They invited me to make their cottage my home. I took my meals at the officers' club. With me were the Superintendent of Schools, the principal of the high school, and the captain of the Philippine constabulary, three fine men —and all of them, like myself, lonesome. While they drowned their loneliness in whiskey, I drowned mine in religion. Every evening at five when the other Americans were at MacSmith's store for their evening comforter, I would climb Signal Hill, back of my cottage, with nobody but my black dog Tip, and talk to God and the sunset.

The first month in Lanao was the hardest of my life. One evening I was sitting on Signal Hill looking over the province that had me beaten. Tip had his nose up under my arm trying to lick the tears off my cheeks. My lips began to move and it seemed to me that God was speaking.

"My child," my lips said, "you have failed because you do not really love these Moros. You feel superior to them because you are white. If you can forget you are an American and think only how I love them, they will respond."

I answered back to the sunset, "God, I don't know whether you spoke to me through my lips, but if you did, it was the truth. I hate myself. My plans have all gone to pieces. Drive me out of myself and come and take possession of me and think thy thoughts in my mind."

In that terrible, wonderful hour on Signal Hill I became color-blind. Ever since, I have been partial to tan, the more tan the better! Every missionary goes through some such experience as that—or comes home defeated.

My lips spoke again to me:

"If you want the Moros to be fair to your religion, be fair to theirs. Study their Koran with them."

I went down the hill and told some *panditas* (priests) that I wanted to study their Koran. The next day they crowded into my little cottage, each with a Koran under his arm. They were bent upon making a Moslem out of me! So we went to work with great zeal.

A few days later they brought me a pamphlet published by an Islamic propaganda society in India, to show me how to be a good Moslem. It said that Islam has four Holy Books: the Torah, the laws of Moses; the Zabur, the psalms of David; the Kitab Injil, the gospel of Jesus Christ; and the Koran of Mohammed.

I sang the doxology under my breath. They had built a bridge across which I might some day be able to lead them to Christ! I said to them, "I have studied these first three books since I was a boy, and you have studied the Koran. We will exchange our knowledge!"

We began a search for more common ground. They brought me a book that said the Moslems believe Jesus was born of the Virgin Mary, but do not believe he was crucified! "When Jesus was praying in Gethsemane God looked at him and said, 'He never did anything wrong. It would not be just to allow him to die.' So God quickly snatched Jesus up to heaven. Then God came back and snapped his finger and made Judas look like Jesus. So they seized Judas and crucified him as he deserved. Even today Jesus Christ is sitting on a throne at the right hand of God, pleading with God to be merciful to us because we are ignorant. Jesus is our best friend in heaven!" Their book also said that in Medina there are four graves—one the grave of Mohammed, another of Fatima his daughter, the third that of Mohammed's greatest missionary, Omar, and the fourth grave is empty. They are saving it for Jesus, who they think will return to the world and reign for a thousand years and then be buried beside Mohammed.

I did not try immediately to correct their theology. For the time being, I was only too glad they had Jesus beside God, no matter how they got him there.

I soon realized that I must have a more thorough knowledge of the Moro language, so I asked an American officer, Lieutenant Cramer, whether he knew any Moro whom I could trust to teach me. Cramer replied:

"There is a Moro here who was convicted of murder and sentenced to twenty years' imprisonment. I thought this sentence was too heavy, so I helped him appeal to the supreme court on a plea of self-defense. I was dumbfounded when he was acquitted. Pambaya is now my loyal friend, and, if I recommend you to him, he will do anything you say."

So this man Pambaya, who so narrowly escaped spending twenty years in prison, became a close friend and has been the strongest bulwark against all opposition ever since. During the past twelve years he helped us prepare our dictionary and translate thousands of pages into Maranaw, including the *Gospel of Luke* and the *Book of Acts*.

Donato Galia, a Filipino with an M.A. from Teachers College, Columbia University, came to Lanao with his wife to cooperate in our mission. He is a born educator and deserves much credit for the discoveries in literacy that were made that year.

Our murderer friend, Pambaya, began to teach Galia and myself the Maranaw language. Not a page of it had ever been printed. The priest knew Arabic letters, as did some of the *datos* (chiefs), but Arabic was too hard for most people. Galia and I adopted a Roman alphabet, one letter to a sound and only one sound to a letter—perfectly phonetic.

When we tried to write the words we heard, nobody could tell us where one word began and another ended! If I asked Pambaya, "What is the Maranaw word for 'go'?" he did not know. But if I asked how to say, "Where are you going?" he answered at once, "*Andakasoong*." By many trials and errors we discovered that *anda* was "where," *ka* was "you," and *soong* was "go"—"Where you go?" We had to make some hard decisions also about spelling. We decided to use "w" for "oo," pronounced as in "two." Then we always used "u" for the sound of "u" pronounced as in "cup"—never two sounds for the same letter.

In six weeks we had a box ten inches long filled with cards recording thirteen hundred words. The words were in the box but not in our heads! Galia learned much more quickly than I did and was talking to everybody in a few weeks. He was bright and besides he was born with a Filipino language, Visayan, in his mouth. All Filipino and Malay languages seem backwards to us Americans. Instead of "What have you?" they say, "What is had by you?" Instead of "Let me see it" they say, "I will be let by you to have it seen by me." It's easy in Maranaw when you get the knack of thinking in roundabout fashion!

After that night on Signal Hill, when God killed my racial prejudice and made me color-blind, it seemed as though he were working miracles at every turn. Galia and I became positively superstitious about it. We needed a school house. William MacSmith, the rough but bighearted American merchant and liquor dealer, said: "Here is a building nobody is using. I reckon you can buy it for two hundred and fifty dollars. The owner went back to God's country [he meant America, not heaven!]. But anyhow you can use it free while we find out what he wants for it."

Thus we had a huge building that had once been a dance hall and motion picture theater, for two hundred and fifty dollars. Later we got MacSmith's store that had once been a saloon. We "converted" it into a church.

We prayed, "Lord, we are grateful for this big school building. But we need a printing press, too." A friend in Cagayan wrote us a letter:

"You don't need a press, do you? We could sell two presses and lots of type, altogether worth about three thousand pesos, for two hundred and fifty pesos, and Silvino Abaniano, the printer, will come with it." Galia and I nearly wept as we read that letter. "God is working ahead of us," he whispered.

So I took the press and the printer to Lanao. "Where shall we put this press?" I asked Donato. "This old floor will not hold up a thousand-pound machine." We examined our big building and there we discovered a concrete base exactly the right shape and size! "Man," I said to Galia, "God put it here for us, twenty years ago!"

Silvino, the printer, began to set up the first page of Maranaw ever put into type. The Moros buzzed with excited curiosity. None of them could read their own language with our alphabet. When the *imams* (chief priests) saw the Roman letters they insisted that we must have Arabic type, which, they said, was the "holy" script of the Moslems. They had an idea that "Roman" type belonged to the Roman Catholic church—that types went with religions! So our teacher Pambaya wrote our newspaper out in Arabic on stencils that the superintendent of schools lent us. We had Arabic text on one side of each sheet and Roman text on the other. We called it *The Story of Lanao*. Here is a translation of the opening paragraphs:

This is the beginning of a story paper in the Moro language, to be distributed around the four sides of Lake Lanao. All Moros feel delighted because this paper is being started. The leading *datos* will furnish stories for the newspaper, telling of the famous ancestors of early days, and the events in Mecca and other important places.

Our paper will also be helpful for business. It will tell the price of rice, corn, beans, various kinds of cloth and thread, of silk and woven hemp, of lumber, brass, silver and gold articles, and betel nuts.

At last the great day came when we were ready to distribute the first issue. I wrote my father all about it:

February 16, 1930

Tomorrow morning will be an important morning in the history of this province, I believe, for we are going to distribute our first paper. Personally, I am not very well pleased with its appearance. We tried to stencil on newsprint, and the ink came through so much that the printing on the other side is not clear. But the Moros who have seen the proof copies are as pleased as though it were bound in gold! They all prophesy that our paper will be a grand success. I hope so, for it involves enough labor to deserve results! We had first to find something they would like; then we had to put it into Maranaw in Roman letters, which has never been done before; then we had to have Pambaya write it in Arabic letters, and a priest had to decide whether it could be understood, and another priest copied it off on a stencil.

Now we have to teach everybody how to read the paper. No Moro but Pambaya can read the side with Roman letters. We have prepared a chart full of short sentences with very large letters. To make this the Superintendent of Schools lent us his box of hand-printing letters. We did our best to teach some Moros these sentences but it hasn't worked well, so Galia and I have gone into a huddle to devise some better way. We revised and re-revised, and shortened and re-shortened our charts until there was nothing else we could think of to do. We asked the Moros to help us and tried out all the ideas that they submitted. They are helping us look for "key words" that will contain all their twelve consonants. They found some rather good "keys," but we are seeking better ones. We keep telling ourselves that this chart must be worked over like an automobile road, until every step is smooth and the grade so easy that the poorest car could slip along without getting stuck or even jolted. The teacher corresponds to the chauffeur. All he needs to do is to learn to keep the car on the road and to regulate his speed and the road will carry him through. This is our ideal.

«««»»»

Thus we were stumbling into the beginnings of a literacy campaign—although this was the farthest thing in the world from our intentions. Galia and I had come intending to start a teachers' normal school. We had never dreamed of teaching the ABC's to adults! But one of the lessons every missionary must learn is to be adaptable, to give up his cherished dreams, and do whatever he finds can be done. This crashing of our plans was harder on poor Galia than on me, for he had spent a year in Teachers College writing a thesis on a normal school for Moros! But the doors opened so wide for a literacy campaign that neither Galia nor I had time to weep over shattered hopes.

One of these doors had been opened by General Pershing, twenty-five years before, when he gave a gold-headed cane to Dato Pandi-in, who ever after was a loyal friend to Americans. In 1941 I carried an ebony and ivory cane to General Pershing as a return gift from Dato Pandi-in. General Bullard opened another door. He studied the Koran until he knew it so well that he surprised the Moslem scholars. A terrible cholera epidemic was killing the Moros but no American soldiers were stricken. Bullard told a one-eyed Moro *hadji*[1] named Kakairan that the water contained little devils, "just as the Koran said," and that the Americans roasted the little devils to death over a fire. The *hadji* took the secret back to his people, the cholera stopped, and America had made one more friend.

When, twenty-five years later, General Bullard's one-eyed friend, Hadji Kakairan, heard of our literacy campaign, he came over from Tamparan bringing his nephew, Gani Noor, whom he offered me as a teacher. Gani Noor became our first Moro literacy expert. How General Bullard's study of the Koran bore fruit thirty years later is revealed in a letter written to my father during my first spring in Lanao:

May 14, 1930

I have just been having one of the most marvelous times of my life—with four Moros, my fine young teacher, Gani Noor, and three of his friends, one named Kakairan, a prominent *hadji*. They have been traveling over this province telling the people that I am the Moros' friend and will help them. One *hadji* asked me why I had come to help the Moros, so I told him:

"I have but one life to live. If I were to acquire a mil-

[1] One who has made the pilgrimage to Mecca.

lion pesos I could not take them with me to heaven. All we ever take with us to heaven is the gratitude of people we have helped; and I think the Moros need a friend at this time.

"You have been helping me in Lanao, for here I have learned that 'Moslem' means 'one who does the will of God in every smallest detail,' and since I have been here I have been trying harder than ever before in my life to keep God in my mind all day. Wherever I find a man like yourself who is trying to submit to the will of God, then he is my dearest friend. You and I shall be friends forever."

The *hadji* replied, "Although you may say you wish to learn about Islam from us, you tell us more about Islam than we have ever heard before."

To my amazement he shamelessly wiped tears from both his eyes with his sleeve. Then I came in for the most astounding bombardment of compliments that I have ever heard or hope to hear. There were too many for me to remember, but here are a few samples:

"Your words are like luscious fruit, which make us want more. We hope that you will promise to live among us forever. We will write our friendship upon iron."

These people here need a friend, and that is why they talk like this.

«‹«›»›

The next day I was still full of open-eyed amazement as I wrote:

Such a marvelous morning that I have almost lost my breath! Gani Noor called together all the leading priests and sultans and *hadjis* and *datos* of Lanao. The governor came and made a welcoming speech. The program lasted for hours. I do not know exactly what they all thought, but I tried through Gani as interpreter to make them all understand that while I knew nothing much about Islam, I was anxious to do the will of God and believed God wanted me in Lanao. They all promised to study how to read and write and to bring their children and buy our newspaper.

Never, it seems to me, was there such evidence that God was doing nine-tenths of the work. Gani Noor seems to be the man God has been preparing for just this work.

During the long forenoon of speeches and questions from these leading Moros, I spent my time thinking of God. I felt that something would go wrong if I let up for a minute. As a result, this had been perhaps the most successful day in keeping God in mind since we began the experiment in March.

Gani Noor and I have nearly finished with the translation of the epic song (*darangan* is what the Moros call it) of the famous ancient Moro hero, Bantugan. Gani Noor tells me that this song is learned by heart by thousands of people. Indeed, in every home the mothers lull their children to sleep with it, and the old men sing it far into the night. At every fiesta and at every wedding, able reciters repeat this tale by the hour.

It is hard to preserve the original beauty in the translation. I am finding it especially difficult to throw into choice English the statement that "Bantugan expectorates a stream of red betel-nut juice." I cannot find any English word that makes this act seem noble; I fear it may detract from your sense of awe at the hero. If we all chewed tobacco or betel nut, we might feel differently. Perhaps I shall take the liberty of omitting the betel nut from the translation, for the rest of the poem possesses restrained dignity like the *Iliad* and *Odyssey*. It ends in a manner that would be a true and thrilling climax to a Moslem, but which I fear cannot be used by the public schools, for Bantugan triumphantly returns from a great fight bringing fifty wives with him! If this poem is to become literature in Christian lands, it will need a little expurgating —although we have never expurgated the scandal about Solomon's seven hundred wives.

When you realize that the unwritten lyric and epic poetry sung by the Moros would make thousands of printed pages, you see that this work of recording becomes highly important to them. It is also important to anthropology as the only survival of the ancient Filipino literature. When Spanish friars reached the Philippines, they stamped out with fire and sword all the folklore of the Filipinos—but they could not stamp out the Moros or their culture. That this Moro folklore is ancient is proved by its strange obsolete language and by the fact that the ideas go back to a period long before the Moslem religion reached the Philippines. The heroes worshipped the spirits of rocks, clouds, and crocodiles and never mentioned God or Mohammed. So we are at last bringing to light something that has been hidden in Lanao for perhaps a thousand years.

June 1, 1930

Six months since I came to Lanao! How fast time flies when one is busy! And I am busy! For now that the Moros have become fast friends, I have little time to myself. They are here morning, noon, and afternoon—fortunately not yet at night. They are afraid of ghosts, and Galia and I are careful not to change that belief!

This forenoon after church, when I wanted to sleep for a few minutes, there was a rap at my door and in walked three distinguished *gooros* (teachers of Islam), and with them three other men. They came, so they said, to pay me a visit on Sunday because all my time was taken during the week and they were afraid I was working too hard. It did not strike them as rather funny to come and awaken me from sleep in order to tell me that they were afraid I was overtired. But I saw the funny side of it, for they were so kindly about it.

I told these religious teachers, "I am trying a little experiment with myself today to see how many minutes I can keep my mind on God, and how many minutes I forget him in spite of myself."

One of the *gooros* replied, "Any man who tries to remember God all the time is not only a good Moslem but he is like Mohammed himself, and when he dies he will be carried up to the seventh heaven."

Then he added what to me was the most pathetic word of all, "We never heard anybody talk like this before, and so we have decided to make you our leader in religion because you are always giving us the loveliest things in the Koran."

"I learned all these things from Jesus," I said. "Jesus and Mohammed agreed that we must do God's will."

"Yes," said the delighted *gooros*, "they said the very same words."

Does it not seem to you that we are getting somewhere when we can have the strong moral backing of all the leading priests and *datos* in Lanao, and can tell them that these ideals are the ideals that we learned from Jesus? Doesn't this justify the method of approach we are trying?

Just at noon today a Moro from Togaya—where all the fighting has taken place during the past few weeks —came to ask us to establish a school there so that the people might learn good customs and stop fighting. Then, to my great surprise, he produced a New Testament and said he wanted to study it and that he wanted to have a copy in Maranaw. I promised that some day we would print it, and now we must make good.

«« «» »»

Excerpts from letters written during the following year reveal the new problems that were arising and give the high points of our progress. I have not attempted to give their respective dates, for they form a running narrative of events.

Our problem is now going to be to print enough literature in Maranaw to keep up with the demand. This week a man came and asked whether the next issue of our magazine was out, and when I offered him a back number he said proudly, "I have read all the old ones and everything else your press has printed in our language." Is there another press in the world that can boast that anybody has read everything it has turned out? Here, many Moros have done so. But that is not saying very much, for our total output to date is about twenty pages!

When one sees the vile trash that appears in some of the books and magazines in English that reach these outposts of civilization, one feels sure we can make better Moros out of those who never learn to read English than out of those who acquire a taste for this low reading. So perhaps we may be able to mold this Moro nation far more than we realize through the pages we shall print and circulate among the people.

Two Moros just came in to show me how they are learning to read. Very, very slowly but correctly one read a paragraph; perhaps in another month he will attain fair speed. He has passed the first, and hardest, achievement, for he knows that letters can be so pronounced together that they form themselves into words and convey the ideas that he wants to express.

During the past months we have devised a system that is so easy that the brightest Moros can repeat every letter within ten minutes. We start with three words that contain all the consonants used in the Maranaw language. These three words are as familiar to them as "mother," "hand," and "work" are to us.

They are *Malabanga,* name of a town in Lanao; *karatasa,* paper; *paganada,* study or learn. We cut the words up like this:

ma	la	ba	nga
ka	ra	ta	sa
pa	ga	na	da

Then we begin with *ma ma,* which means man; *a ma,*

which means father; *ma la,* which means big, and so on.
The combination of these consonants with the other vowels
in the language is a simple additional step. Learning to
read from the chart is so easy that the most stupid person
can do it.[1] And they love it so much they hardly give us
time to eat.

It is like a miracle for a man who never knew a letter to
walk out of our school in an hour able to read a whole page
of his own language with Roman letters. We see that
miracle happen over and over, every day. But the joy of
seeing people learning ten times as fast as they expected
to learn and all set up about their own brilliance does not
lose its edge.

Mr. Galia says that he taught nine Moros to read in a
half hour. That is better than any record that I have thus
far made with a large group. A half dozen Moros interrupted this letter. They came in and said they could not
wait until tomorrow but had to be taught right away! They
had only an hour to spare and wanted all the education
they could get in that time. So I have stopped this letter to
teach them. While I concentrated on one of them, the rest
listened. They have just left the house. I do not expect you
to believe me, but here is the fact: this man had finished
reading three pages of our newspaper, and could read
everything I put before him with fair speed. One hour!
Every time that happens I feel as though a miracle had
happened. It is possible only because these people are
hungry mentally and spiritually.

Nine-tenths of our job is sitting close beside the people

[1] See chart on p. 36.

FIRST MARANAW READING CHART

Lesson I

a	ma	la	ba	nga
i	mi	li	bi	ngi
o	mo	lo	bo	ngo
u	mu	lu	bu	ngu

ma ma	a ma	la la	a la	ma la	la ma
man	father	to pat	God	large	yard

mi mi	a mi	li li	a li	li ma	li o
girl	our	name	name	hand	outside

mo mo	a mo	lo lo	a lo	ma lo	o lo
chewed	monkey	dull	hello	pretty	head

ba ba	ba ba i	la ba	ba la	ba li	ba lo
short	woman	profit	pair	a receipt	clang

bi bi	bi ba i	la bi	i bi	o bi	lo bi
duck	push	more	itch	a vegetable	cocoanut

bo bo	ba bo	la bo	bo la	bu la	bu l
to pour	aunt	prefer	ball	wide	smoke

nga nga	ba nga	bo nga	lu nga	ma nga	o nga
open mouth	island	fruit	plural	a fly	fruit

ngi ngi	la ngi	li ngi	lu ngi	lu ma	lu mi
corner of mouth	wait	to turn	allow	smooth	make flat

who flock to us and getting thrills of delight with them as they emerge from ignorance. Just this morning we drove forty kilometers, stopping to teach crowds of Moros and to distribute the newest chart. The speed with which the people learned was even more astonishing to them than it was to me, for they had not had opportunity to see the thing happen before.

Yesterday an old *hadji* came to see me, and though he thought he was too old to learn to read a new way, we assured him that it was easy and he started. We kept him roaring with laughter and in fifteen minutes he knew every letter and could read. A letter a minute! When he went up the road he was still laughing and reading. This sounds incredible, yet we are doing it daily. Fifteen minutes is the time we expect a bright man who knows Arabic letters to require to learn to read Roman letters. Those who never knew how to read anything before require from an hour to a week.

One of the outlaws (I had better not name him for he's now my friend) came at five in the evening and I taught him in a half hour. He was unusually bright and very much pleased with himself, and I praised him and told him I wanted him to be a teacher in his village. When we had finished he took me over where nobody else could hear us and said, "You taught me to read, and you are the best friend I have in the world. I want to do something for you. Is there anybody in Lanao you want me to put out of the way?" I said, "No, thank you, brother. But you are certainly a very big-hearted man. Go home and teach others and that will make me happy."

I have been trying to teach a boy to read this afternoon, but his mind was so slow the task seemed like pouring water into a mosquito net. I often wonder when I am working with a stupid man whether he is worth all this effort. But then when that same man fondly runs his fingers through my hair and fairly beams with gratitude while he calls me "good uncle," I know that a little love is created. If, as we believe, this entire universe is a desperate attempt of love to incarnate itself, then "important duties" that cut us off from helping little people are not duties but sins.

On market day twice a week, I stand from seven to twelve before a chart in the marketplace while people crowd around trying to get near enough to learn to read, always threatening to push me off my stool in their eagerness to be next. I do not see how my teachers get time to record the names of their students; I seldom do.

As I finished breakfast about six-thirty and arose from the table there came a knock at the door. I turned the knob and there crowded into my little house sultans and *hadjis* and *datos*; sixty tried to get in, but some had to stay outside for want of room. They had hired a launch and had come twenty miles to be examined, for they had learned to read Moro with English letters. We marched down the road a mile to our school, and there we spent the whole forenoon in joyously throwing compliments at one another. Everybody in the province seems caught up with the same gladness. They think the whole world will be surprised at their achievement, and I think they are right! This thing may have had parallels, but I have neither seen them nor heard of them. On our school wall is a motto: "In five years, Lanao the most literate province in the Philippines." These men declared, "Less than five years, much less!"

But there is a price to pay for all this—one cannot get any time alone. Three men, very intimate friends and splendid workers, have just been here and in spite of my hints and insistences that I needed to work, they stayed a long time. One of them is writing a letter about our campaign to the President of the United States at this moment; and he did not relent until we promised to translate it into English and send it to President Hoover.

Any executive will say, "You ought to organize your time and have it understood that visitors are welcome only at certain hours." Something, at least, must be done about it; but not something that will nip our tender promising plant in the bud. What a beautiful frail thing it is!

The Moros know that we love them, but they do not realize what a gulf—at least historically—separates us. If they did, would they be so affectionate? Yes, if they knew all, if they knew the love of God in all its wondrous fervor, they would!

And to think that less than a year ago we were writing about "the most difficult place under the American flag, if not in the world"!

I think now that America is the most difficult place in the world, for there you demand ability, unusual ability, while here in Lanao they demand only love.

It is the end of a day as nearly perfect as any I have ever seen, and so I write about it at once. It has been exasperatingly busy, for Moros have come to the house from early morning to dark. They were all so loving and grateful that I think I never saw anything like it before in the whole world. As darkness approached, I sent them home, telling them I must walk off alone. As I climbed Signal Hill, God began to use my tongue to speak to me:

"My child you have at last struck your pace. Here in Lanao you will accomplish something with me for the human race. You will broaden the circle of their minds, which is good, and you will help them to a new comradeship with me, which is the most wonderful thing that can happen to any man. This very minute, while you are walking with me and listening to me, you are doing the last highest thing a human being can ever do. You must not fret because you have not done more in your life. Only live close to me minute by minute as you have done so much of the day today, and what you *are* will speak. You need not worry about what you do, but only what you are. And what you are depends upon whether you *are holding on to me.*"

The Moros come and watch our Sunday services with ever increasing interest and appreciation. To our great delight we have found that they like Jesus. It is Christians they hate because Christians have mistreated and misunderstood them. They love Jesus and claim him for their own. So we are going to try to write a series of tracts on "Jesus as a Good Friend," to be distributed in Maranaw in the marketplace. If we can untangle Christ from the terrible handicap of Christendom, which has kept so many millions from him, we will be doing the Moros a priceless service.

When we came here in 1915 for the first time, we heard an officer say that the only good Moro was a dead one, and I have heard this very statement repeated by government officials this year. Perhaps the only good Moros they come in contact with are dead ones, but our program has attracted a group of young men who in my estimation are as big-hearted and as splendid as any young men you could find in any country. My heart is all bound up with them. I never had friends whom I felt I could rely upon to be more loyal and who understood my own motives better than these Moros. Neither they nor I feel that the boundary of religion or race can keep us apart.

A swift, wonderful year has gone by [I wrote in January, 1931], and yet it would not be counted much of a success in many mission circles. There has not as yet been a single baptism of a Moro. They do not even know that baptism is our custom.

On the other hand, we can claim one victory. Almost one hundred per cent of the Moros are now our friends. It has been encouraging, too, to hear so many visitors in Lanao say, "This is what I call true missionary work!"

Some months ago the Sultan of Samoi collected over a thousand signatures of prominent *datos* and sent them along with a beautiful betel-nut box to Mayor Charles G. Phillips of Montclair, New Jersey. Today Mayor Phillips' reply arrived. I showed it to the men who are helping us make a dictionary, and they were so delighted they could not sit still. Mayor Phillips had pictured "a university to be established at your capital—an institution where boys and girls from all over the island might come for intellectual training, and then go back as teachers to their own localities." These men kept saying, "My goodness, that is just the thing. Just think what that would do for Lanao."

Sheik Bogabong, the very highest scholar of all the Moros, came this morning and this afternoon, followed by his retinue, to help us and to discuss religious problems. He is so genuine and friendly and so interested in the quest for God, which means everything to me, that I enjoyed the conversations greatly.

He said that the chief difference between Islam and Christianity was that the Moslem can pray anywhere, while Christians have to go to church! One of my fellow-workers objected to this, and said that I prayed on top of Signal Hill at sunset. Sheik Bogabong replied, "That is just where Mohammed and Jesus liked to pray best—on a hilltop!" Then Campong, my helper, said, "Ah, the Bible and the Koran are much alike on the question of prayer."

Yesterday Effa and I went with Lieutenant Alviola and his wife to Ramain and visited a number of homes. Abolais, the teacher, had a *ba-i* or princess from the royal family read for us in each house. They all could read rapidly and beautifully. It was market day in Ramain and men were learning to read all about the market. Hundreds of men and about fifty women have learned to read here in the past two months.

We all wanted to know how Abolais had secured such a stampede of Ramain ladies to learn to read, so he told us his secret. He had a handsome young man write a love lyric to one of the young ladies who had already learned, telling her that her education made her the most charming lady in Lanao. She read the love song to the other young ladies, and the scramble to learn to read was on—a perfect illustration of the use of love as an educational instrument! When we told the other teachers how Abolais did it, they all declared they would adopt the same method and now we have to print a love lyric every week in *Lanao Progress*.

In the whole province six hundred Maranaw women and girls have thus far been reported as having learned to read. Every week some high *dato* brings his daughter and asks us to keep her in our school, which we are not yet equipped to do. You see what a wonderful opportunity is opening here.

We now have twenty literacy teachers, most of them high school students and some of them graduates, scattered through the main districts. Their average pay is ten dollars a month. Besides these twenty who are in the employ of the *madrasa*, as our folk school is called, there are at least fifty others who are doing more or less regular teaching without pay. They reported having taught 930 this month, which is at the rate of 11,160 a year.

We have just come home from high adventure in Togaya, the home of notorious outlaws. It is our first visit since the soldiers destroyed their stone fort. Mr. McKinley, who was with us, tried to become friendly with one *imam* (religious leader), but received only black looks in return. This man was probably a close friend of the outlaws. As soon as we pulled out our lesson sheets there was a buzz of excitement. The old *imam* suddenly became friendly and said he had heard of the "American *madrasa*." Every person in the party was soon surrounded by a crowd of Moros, all of them learning to read. When you consider that they burned down the only school they ever had, ten years ago, you can see what this new doorway to civilization may mean to them.

Campong Basman said, as we were leaving Togaya,

"Our poor Moro people do not know in which direction to go and are in need of leaders. They follow anybody who knows what to do."

Campong is a keen-minded young Moro who graduated from Muños Agricultural College and began to teach, but was dismissed from the Bureau of Education for carrying firearms without a license. He is a tireless worker and a high-grade translator. He has just completed the translation of a little booklet on the care of babies, and has translated about a hundred pages of the Old Testament. From our pulpit on Sunday morning, he has been reading the stories of the Prophets to the Moros.

The Christian Endeavor meeting is just out. Down the street tonight goes somebody singing and whistling, "Out of the darkness into the light, Jesus, I come, Jesus, I come." It sounds like Campong Basman. Though still a Moslem, he takes a leading part in Christian Endeavor every week.

I think we could have imposing statistics in the way of church membership this year, but if we did so we might sacrifice the wonderful good will that now exists toward our enterprise. If we can be of great service to the Moros during the next four or five years educationally, medically, and in other ways, then they will think of our Christianity in terms of loving service rather than in terms of doctrine. Hitherto, Christians have seemed chiefly enemies of Mohammed and Islam. We do not want to be thought of as enemies of any other religion, but as lovers of all men.

Last Sunday was a turning point for our church here. We abandoned our room at the military camp and went to the Moro school in Dansalan to hold our Christian services. The windows were all filled with Moros listening to the service from start to finish. I spent a couple of minutes preaching to the Moros in their own language. What I said was about as follows:

"Friends, we use a different language and worship with somewhat different forms, but we worship the same God. These songs that we sing today could all be sung by you with as much earnestness as they are sung by us. The story of Joseph, which we read, is well known to you, for Joseph is one of your great prophets. Come in and worship with us if you wish. We call you our dear friends."

The life of the pioneer missionary can be thrilling! Never did I enjoy any other work as I do this. It is literally true that the missionaries on the very front lines are the ones who are getting the greatest fun out of their experiences. If anybody is going to be a missionary, let him plunge into the farthest frontiers. Never pity Livingstone again. Envy him, loneliness, malaria, and all!

Livingstone never had an experience like mine yesterday! We have five automobiles in Dansalan now, great curiosities to the people across the lake, where there are neither roads nor autos. Kakai (pronounced Cockeye) Dagalangit brought six of his thirteen wives, with their daughters and maid-servants, yesterday to see our auto and beg for a ride. So fourteen queens and princesses piled into our Ford, two or three deep, every princess saturated with perfume from Cairo. They giggled incessantly until we reached the corkscrew road down the mountain, when some of them began to get sick. A few got out, two leaned out, and one leaned on my shoulder. I did not hesitate for an instant to turn homeward, for there was a hole in one tire and I trembled for it every minute. Think of fourteen sick royal ladies, a flat tire, and no spare! Harems have lost their glamour.

Everywhere I turn I see people teaching each other to read, or else reading the papers that we have printed.

We have doubled our force of Moro typesetters, all inexperienced but eaten up with zeal. They are putting forced draught on our printing presses—we bought another old press—so that we may catch up with the rising demand for literature.

Yesterday a young man came and said, "We have now read everything you have printed. Are you finished with a new issue of the paper?"

"Not until next Monday."

He began to walk the floor in consternation as he said, "What will the young ladies do? They will be discouraged if they have nothing to read. They will finish this paper in a day. Then what?"

Then what! That is the question we are now trying to solve!

Lieutenant Carlton of the U. S. Army and Mrs. Carlton have been visiting Lanao for a week. They were deeply interested in our program and spent a long while watching us teach the Moros to read. They watched us make these large charts by hand, since of course our presses are too small for them. The day before they left, Lieutenant Carlton said, "Mrs. Carlton and I have noticed how much you need more charts, and how slow the present process is. If you will give us a sample of just what you want, we will make them on better paper than you have so that they will last longer; we will send you one thousand."

I visualized what it meant in an instant—a large lovely chart in every chieftain's house—and was so happy I felt stunned.

"Lieutenant," I said, "this means that we shall win! This will be the most literate province in the Philippines in five years—and perhaps the most literate in Asia." So every day has new wonders; it *is* God who is doing this.

Before I opened my front door this morning I heard some men outside. One was a *dato* from Waw, a distant corner of the province. He said, "We have no public school in our district. The people are all ignorant, not even one man who can teach the rest of us. We want you to send us a teacher."

"There is no money to send you a teacher," I replied. "But Mr. Presidente (he was the mayor of his town), suppose you learn right now and go back and teach the people yourself."

So he went at it and in an hour he could read—slowly, it is true, but perfectly. Then he started in to learn to write. We teach them to print their letters, so they are easy to learn. He went away with a large, brilliantly decorated chart in his hand, a diploma under his arm, and a broad grin on his face. "I graduated from the *madrasa* yesterday," he will say when he gets home. "Now I am your teacher."

This morning early a group of *datos* came to give us land. They wanted us to have a beautifully situated piece of land, which we had regarded as the most desirable in Dansalan, for a Moro girls' dormitory and school. They told me that they absolutely would not sell it to anybody else for it was too precious, but for our school they wanted to give it without a cent. And they were so excited about it that one of them said, "If anybody else ever tries to build a house on that land, we will murder him!"—and they meant it. These fellows have pretty tough ways with their enemies, but what marvelous friends they can be! The wife of one owner crowded up and cried in a high voice, "I told my husband if he did not give that property to you, I would cut his throat while he was asleep." The husband smiled proudly. It was his wife's gentle hint that she agreed with him entirely.

The financial situation in America has hit some of our supporters so hard that I shall have to cut my budget to less than one-half. I have gone over our meager resources and looked for money until I am about sick, but will have to drop twelve of our staff and cut the salaries of all the rest. This will reduce our total budget by one hundred dollars a month. I have worked over these names a hundred different ways to make the operation as painless as possible—they are such splendid, loyal fellows. Tomorrow they must be told; it will be a very critical day. If I fail in tact and wisdom everything may smash up, or worse. When one has a painful job like this to face, one needs to be alone. I am really scared about that meeting, and feel like a cur after all those boys have done.

I am so keyed up this evening that I cannot relax. It has been a wonderful and a terrible day. I have had nothing in all my life like it.

I tried to prepare our teachers for the shock by giving them the Friendship Treasure Chests filled with school supplies that were sent from the children in America.

Then I told the teachers to write letters to those who sent the chests, explaining our terrible dilemma and the necessity of cutting our expenses in half. They all promised to write.

Then we heard the reports of their literacy work. Man alive, some of them made me weep! I know from experience what labor is involved in teaching fifty, sixty, eighty people, one by one, how to read. One man, Santos Gangawa, taught forty-one women and seventy-one men to read during this one month. How the crowd applauded his description! Something in my eyes would not behave, and all over that room I felt the same deep emotion almost ready to break out. The room became tense and silent as man after man came forward with his magnificent achievement for the salvation of his province.

I felt swept on by a power that I could neither explain nor control. I was a little part of it, and so were all the others. I know it was the spirit of God in a strange new form. At last the names of all who had learned to read were counted and there were 1,521, over three hundred of them women. Then fifty-one young men arose and volunteered to be teachers, making one hundred and ten volunteers in all. I felt as though I were passing through an incredible dream. Somebody moved that we have a gigantic fiesta, and the sultans and *datos* who crowded that room voted with a mighty roar that a month from today Dansalan is to see such a fiesta as was never seen here in Lanao. And all that amazing morning a tragic secret was in my breast and I was afraid.

Then came the terrible afternoon. I had to call in the paid teachers and tell them one by one that I could not pay them any longer. These same magnificent fellows that had felt such a thrill in the morning had to hear that my money was exhausted. I told them the truth, that it would be much easier to jump in the lake than to face them with this news. I expected some of them, at least, to go into a rage, but they saw that I was suffering and so they rose to it like men. Some of them hung their heads and turned pale, but not a man showed any resentment. Because they saw how sick I was about it myself I think they learned a new sympathy, and we are better friends because of the things we are suffering together.

«««»»»

When I told Kakai Dagalangit I had no money to pay the teachers, he said: "This campaign shall not stop for lack of money. It is Lanao's only hope—if it stops, we are lost. Everybody who learns has got to teach. If he doesn't, I'll kill him!"

So in our darkest hour this big, fierce, brilliant-eyed chieftain of all southern Lanao invented the method of "each one teach one," which has since gone around the world!

CHAPTER THREE

The "Each One Teach One" Idea Spreads

IN THE ten years following the opening of the Lanao Station the attitude of the Moros toward Christianity swung from one pole to the other. It was unmitigated hatred when we arrived; love, good will, and cooperation when we departed. As one after another of the younger generation was baptized during the last two years not a word of opposition reached our ears. The members of our church were trying to keep God in their thoughts every minute of the day so that, as they said, "the Moros will see Christ in us." This was why we developed the "Game with Minutes," which is our adaptation of Brother Lawrence's effort to practise the presence of God all day long. The daughter of the Sultan, who was attending our girls' school, said openly that she was going to be baptized. The Sultan himself had too many wives to become a Christian, but he always came and had his picture taken right in the center of our church photographs.

"LIGHTNING LITERACY" STRIKES THE NORTH

The beginning of this Lanao transformation had repercussions in other parts of the Philippines almost from the first. In 1930 the pastors of the United Evangelical Church of the Philippines came to Dansalan for a retreat to pray and plan. Before they left they made a Cebuan chart, like our Maranaw chart, and just as easy to learn. Our printer, Silvino Abaniano, himself a Cebuano, worked night and day to print the new chart so that every preacher could take a supply home with him. These preachers went away in high spirits and started literacy campaigns in other parts of Mindanao and in the central Philippines.

Then came one of those miraculous interventions that make me sure God is working for the forgotten illiterates. It happened (or did it just happen?) that my old friend Dr. Sidney L. Gulick, of the Committee on World Friendship among Children in New York, thinking I still lived in Manila, appointed me American representative to help distribute the twenty-eight thousand beautiful Friendship Treasure Chests sent by the children of America to the children of the Philippines. This was the third and last of Dr. Gulick's great friendly gift adventures. The first, in 1926-27, was when American children sent thousands of dolls to Japan. These were distributed in nearly every village in Japan amid a great wave of pro-Americanism. If we had sent more "ships of friendship," we might not be at war with Japan today. The second, in 1928-29, a shower of schoolbags from the children of America to the children of Mexico, had great influence in counteracting the Mexican's dislike for Yankee *gringos*. The Friendship Chests for the Philippine children were very attractive. They were of metal, decorated with pictures of Washington, Rizal, Columbus, Magellan, gods of the sea, and maps of the world, in imitation of ancient Spanish treasure chests. Inside they were crammed with a variety of articles that the children of America had thought would please the children of the Philippines.

At the end of 1930 I spent ten days in Manila helping direct the formal reception of the Chests and the great celebration before Rizal's monument on the Luneta. This responsibility brought me into contact with many officials from the Governor-General to the Director of Education. All of them were interested in literacy.

It was while I was in Manila that Mr. E. K. Higdon, then secretary of the National Christian Council, arranged for me to make an exploratory literacy expedition through the northern Philippines. So the following October found me again aboard ship on the way from Mindanao to Manila. In the midst of a storm—and with everybody seasick!—I tried to write my father about the start of my voyage:

October 18, 1931

I am on my way to the northern part of the Philippines to help prepare lessons like those we made for the Moros in several Filipino dialects.

We are now out from behind the shelter of Mindanao and the waves are becoming uncomfortable. A sudden storm has struck us. Bump, rattle, bang go the doors. Good-by until it is over.

Three hours later: The tables are tied against the wall. The floor is streaked with rain, which is driving through the closed windows. At this moment a window was shaken loose with a loud clatter. There goes the hardest shock we have had yet. I wonder how much water poured into the lower deck of this little steamer.

Mindanao Sea is an ugly piece of water, because storms like this pile up against the tidal currents that pour in from the Pacific Ocean to the China Sea.

The wind howls worse every minute. I wonder whether the hearts of all the passengers are behaving as strangely as mine. I am reminded of Bob's remark after he was in an airplane: "I wasn't scared, but my stomach was." I wonder whom I shall see first in heaven if this ship capsizes or goes down. I read somewhere that if one prays for others he can forget himself. Can I pray for all the passengers on this ship while we toss about on this enraged sea?

Yes! It works! Praying for others has brought my heart back to its normal beat again. There goes a wave clear over the ship, but I have not stopped praying for the Filipinos and my heart behaves perfectly.

The captain has surrendered to the storm and is trying to keep it on our stern. We must be going at a terrific rate, yet the spray blows over the ship from stern to stem each time we pitch up, down, up.

Two hours later: Behind Siquijor Island—safe, and almost calm.

≪≪≪≫≫≫

When we reached Manila, there on the dock was the energetic Mr. Higdon, who hurried me to Union Seminary, to the University, to the Bureau of Education, and to the newspaper reporters. The report went over Manila that we could teach people to read in a day—some said an hour; and an article entitled "Lightning Literacy" appeared in the best journal in the Islands. It was a month before I had time to do any writing. Paragraphs from my next two letters to my father reveal what had been accomplished:

To date we have completed charts in nine languages—Visayan, Tagalog, Ibanag, Ilocano, Gaddang, Isinay, Pampangan, Pangasinan, and Bicol. It is proving easier than we had feared to find the key words for each of these languages. We have trained a hundred and fifty young people to teach and have given them certificates.

A young Kalinga at the American Bible Society helped prepare a chart in his dialect. The Kalinga tribe lives in the northernmost mountains of Luzon. My curiosity was excited by the striking differences between Kalinga and all other Philippine dialects. It has no "r" as the others have; also, unlike the others, it does have the letter "j." Governor Early, who lived among them for several years, has an explanation. He says that an ancient colony of Japanese was driven into the mountains and intermingled with the natives, introducing Japanese sounds. Certainly their features bear more resemblance to those of the Japanese than do those of any of their neighbors.

We are taking steps to teach illiterates in the leper colony on Culion Island. This will bring the Bible, and thus comfort and enrichment of life, to those pitiful unfortunates—there are six thousand of them—who are least able to care for themselves.

«««»»»

During this tour I felt more strongly than ever that we could sweep the world with this scheme of key-word teaching if it were not for one obstacle—the spelling of the English language! If we spelled English phonetically, American children could be taught to read in a week. We needed only a day with the Philippine dialects. I can see only one thing to do—start a strike against the way English is misspelled—become a spelling Bolshevist! I suppose that unless we revolt we shall be handing on this same accursed orthography to our children, and our children's children, to the crack of doom.

THE TIDE SWEEPS ON IN LANAO

Back in Lanao, in the meantime, larger and larger numbers of Moros had been learning to read. We made a "literacy thermometer" to place on our school wall. It was ten feet high and recorded percentages from zero to one hundred. The left side showed the literacy percentages of the leading nations of the world; the right side, where Lanao stood each month. In 1931 the "mercury" —red paint!—showed a literacy of twenty per cent. It had grown steadily since our campaign had begun in January, 1930, when we estimated the literacy of Lanao to be four per cent. A year later it had risen to eight per cent, and during 1931 it increased at the rate of one per cent a month.

Several of the little boys became as expert in teaching as any of the men, and we could not refuse them certificates when their work was perfect. Besides, they were favorites with the women, who were timid about allowing any men except their husbands to teach them. Hundreds of women in all parts of the province were being taught by small boys, while thousands more were learning to read from other women. We knew that we could not get one hundred per cent of the men unless we got one hundred per cent of the women.

I have never found such genuinely grateful people as the Moros. We lived under a spell of continuous benediction. Nor have I ever felt so utterly safe in my life. I knew that if anybody tried to harm us, he would first have to deal with a hundred thousand Moros. They have qualities of fidelity and independence that every American honors. I am frank to confess that I lost my heart to the Moros.

Every Friday, in the Moslem mosques, Hadji Pambaya preached the ideals that he learned in our mission. He told the Moros that God expected them to be honest; that it was God's will for every man to forget his own selfish interests and devote his life to serving his fellowman. The *hadji* returned from the mosque one day and told me that he had been pleading with the Moros to resist the idea of opening a cabaret, as some had planned to do. "We must not adopt everything we see in Western countries," he told them, "for many things there are bad. Though they call themselves Christian, some Western countries do not follow the teachings of Nabi Isa (Jesus). The Protestant mission is opposed to the cabaret. We are not going to admit that our religion does not have ideals as high as the ideals of these missionaries, are we?"

In the spring of 1932 I was filled with joy by the arrival of a staunch Moro Christian, and I wrote my father of what it would mean for our work!

March 13, 1932

The Moro Christian from Jolo, Matias Cuadra, whose story, you will remember, is in *Seven Thousand Emeralds*, is here with his family. He has come to work with us! Today he preached his first sermon. The church—the one that was once a saloon—was crowded, with more Moslems than Christians. Matias produced a profound impression as he talked about "Youth Movements Around the World." He made the babies cry with his mighty shout, while the rest of the audience gasped and trembled. As I sit tonight I can remember nearly every word he said—sure proof that he said it well.

The first day Matias arrived he began to mix with the people of the town. To the delight of the *hadjis*, he talked with them in Malayan, which is almost as sacred to them as Arabic. Mrs. Cuadra has a sweet voice, and is teaching the Moros Christian tunes. The new day has dawned for Lanao, and we are unutterably grateful.

«««»»»

Another very important event took place that spring. The new governor-general of the Philippines, Theodore Roosevelt, Jr., visited Lanao and made a lasting impression upon the Moros and upon our school.

We went down to Iligan to meet him as he came in on the boat. Fine arches had been erected over the entrance to the dock, and the people of Iligan presented him with the "key to the city." He lived up to all their highest expectations for cordiality, making them feel that he was really glad to meet each person who came to shake hands with him. When he was given the key, he made a short but telling address.

The following day Mr. Roosevelt came to our school in Dansalan intending to stay only a few minutes, but he stayed half an hour. He showed deep interest and made some very helpful suggestions. He was enthusiastic about the eighteen Societies of Educated Youth that we had organized around Lake Lanao, and listened attentively while some of these young Moros told him that they were meeting every week to answer the question, "How can we help our town, our province, our country, and the world?"

"This is not mere theory," they told him. "We have found thirty needs in our province and we have set our shoulders with all our power to meet these needs. Each of us has charts in his home and has promised to teach as many people as he can. We are distributing seeds around the four parts of Lanao. We are showing people how to keep well. We are encouraging people to send their children to school. Hitherto we have thought the only use of education was to become a clerk or errand boy in a government office, but we have discovered so many ways to be useful to humanity that we are intoxicated with enthusiasm."

Their eyes flashed and their voices had a new ring. These boys were dreaming dreams far beyond the borders of Lanao. They were tingling with eagerness to do something for all the world. One day I had read to them from Professor Fleming's book, *Marks of a World Christian*, that "two out of three inhabitants of our globe have still to be taught to read and write. The United States may send its hundreds of teachers to the Philippines and make those islands a world model for educational progress, but there are a billion more who need this help."

"Boys," I had burst forth, "you and I are in the biggest undertaking we ever heard of. This book says that two-thirds of the people of the world cannot yet read. Let's start a world campaign! Tell the literacy teachers I'll have my eye on them and very likely some may be called to foreign countries to establish literacy campaigns like ours. Write to the *datos* and tell them that I believe that a world literacy movement is beginning in Lanao and I am on fire with the idea."

The boys had caught fire, too. We started at once to see what improvements we could make in our chart and in our methods of teaching. When we finished there was roaring in my ears the assurance that we were going to arouse the enthusiasm of many leaders in this literacy enterprise, and that it would sweep around the world.

We had made a large map of the world, with Dansalan, Lanao, Mindanao, in the very center. Whenever a letter came from some other part of the world, we would stick on a bright red silk thread running from that country to Lanao Province. The *datos* would come and ask what the threads meant, and while we explained to them, they would cluck their tongues and say, "See how important we are becoming all over the world! We'll certainly have to go and help those other people." How their eyes popped when Governor-General Roosevelt studied that map and asked me to send charts of Moro lessons to Puerto Rico, where he had been governor-general before coming to the Philippines.

At one of our meetings, called to enable the young men to explain to the *datos* about our dream of helping the world, Kakai Dagalangit stood up and said, "If we are going to do that for the world, we will first have to change our name. People think that Moros do nothing but murder and steal and spit betel nut. But now we have stopped being foolish and are getting educated. Why, most of us can read already! Please go to Manila and ask Governor-General Roosevelt to change our name. Tell him to call us 'Islam,' for that means we are trying to do the will of God."

Some of our young men wanted to be baptized, but we were leaning over backward in that respect to avoid fanatical opposition. So far we had baptized only one Moro boy and two Moro girls. We had achieved something, however, that should not be under-estimated. There was a

new friendliness toward our religious services so marked
that the Moros came and watched us worship with open
sympathy. I returned their visits by accepting their invitations to worship with them in their mosques every Friday noon. And after the prayers were finished, we would
sit around in a circle in the center of the mosque, talking
about the prophets and Nabi Isa Rokola (Jesus Christ)—
ours and theirs!

THE SECOND LITERACY CAMPAIGN IN THE NORTH

In the autumn of 1932 I was off on another tour to
the north, to the island of Luzon—a journey that lasted
until almost Christmas. Early in my travels Mrs. Josefa
Jara Martinez, one of those wonderful Protestant Filipina
leaders, took me to Welfareville, where she conducted
government homes for delinquent minors, orphans, and
destitute aged. I trained about twenty teachers, and later
they sent me a splendid letter, pledging themselves to
teach four illiterate inmates each before I returned in two
weeks' time.

At the invitation of Colonel Santos, Director of Prisons,
I went with Dr. George William Wright to Bilibid Prison
in Manila, where a large majority of the prisoners were
unable to read or write. The Director said the prison
needed to teach literacy because it would give the prisoners
mental occupation and make them better citizens when
they were discharged. I stayed there over seven hours—
my longest prison sentence to date!—and trained about
forty prisoners, most of them Moros, to teach. One pris-

oner told me, "Half the murders in the Philippines are committed by your Moro friends!"

At the church in Cavite, I taught a servant girl to read, and the next day she taught the entire chart beautifully to another servant, in front of some thirty people. She was so overcome with joy that she wiped the tears from her eyes with her red handkerchief as she taught. The women who watched her wept, and the men turned their backs or bowed their heads and blew their noses. When the girl finished teaching, the pastor asked us to sing "Praise God from whom all blessings flow," and the meeting turned into a service of thanksgiving. Thereafter Pastor Cruz held literacy classes in that church at five every afternoon and evangelistic campaigns at night. "My little army," he boasted, "will teach five hundred persons within the next year. You'll see!"

We had developed a splendid chart in the Ilocano dialect. The three key words we selected were: *carabasa*—"calabash (squash)"; *mangalata*—"let us take it"; and *nagapada*—"they had a fight." We associated the three words with this story: "Two boys found a 'squash' and said, 'Let us take it'; but 'they had a fight.'" On the chart were pictures of (1) a calabash, (2) two boys running, and (3) pulling each other's hair. Everywhere we traveled in northern Luzon people shouted, *"Carabasa! Mangalata! Nagapada!"* And we shouted back, *"Wen apo!"* which literally is "Yes, sir!" but has the flavor of "Oh, boy, you've said it!"

In Bangued, the capital of the province of Abra, the

presidente was an ex-teacher and deeply interested in literacy. He himself learned our method, then he required his secretary, his clerks, his councilors, the captain of his constabulary, and a number of his lieutenants to learn. I taught practically all the government employees in the town. A map of Bangued with every house drawn in was prepared and hung on the wall of the big, dirty, old *municipio*. The *presidente* and his force, together with the constabulary, planned to visit all the homes, recording the number of male and female illiterates in each house, and then to send teachers to teach in every home. A gold star was to be pasted on each house that became one hundred per cent literate.

At Lagangilang Agricultural School in Abra my heart went out especially to two boys of the primitive Apayao tribe of northern Luzon. They had black tattoos covering their bodies and wore bright red G-strings—a tribal custom. The boys were so eager to learn to teach their people that they would not let me go to lunch; they had heard that I was to leave in an hour and they felt that their learning to teach was infinitely more important than anybody's meal. They said that nobody in their mountain tribe was able to read or write and they made me promise to go to those remote mountains above Baguio to prepare Apayao lessons.

At Baoguen, in Ilocos Sur, fifty people gathered from the hills and mountains, some walking thirty kilometers. We taught twelve who had never read before, and the second day passed six of them as qualified teachers. The whole community was abuzz with excitement. As we ate our dinner we could hear people in the neighboring houses repeating the chart—*carabasa* and all the rest, syllable by syllable. "Nobody in those houses knows how to read," said our hostess.

The *presidente* of San Fernando told me, "In all our family I am the only man who has been able to read. Think what a struggle it has been for me to get an education." He brought his own brother to be taught, and in an hour the brother knew all the syllables and could read very slowly. The man's face was radiant, and the *presidente* was astonished beyond measure. "It took me two years to learn to read even a little English," he said. We all laughed as I patted the young man on the back and said to the *presidente*, "See how much brighter your brother is!"

In all my life I have never engaged in work that brought to the surface so much genuine gratitude and such pathetic longing for help. For thirty years my heart had ached for these multitudes, and now that the way was opened to help them, I was grateful to God beyond words.

I was introduced to the students of Muños Agricultural School by Professor Ambrosio Torres, a fine Christian gentleman, who said, "Boys, do you remember how our martyred hero, Dr. José Rizal, risked his life to return to the Philippines in order to cut the cataracts from his mother's eyes?[1] You can be Rizals and cut the cataracts

[1] See *Seven Thousand Emeralds*, by Frank C. Laubach, pp. 6, 7. New York, Friendship Press, 1929.

of illiteracy from the eyes of your mothers and fathers and neighbors." The effect of this speech was electric. To a man the students promised that when they went home for vacation they would try to teach their relatives and neighbors to read and write.

Upon returning to Manila from this tour through the Ilocos provinces, I found our leading Protestant layman, Jorge Bocobo, president of the University of the Philippines, intensely interested. He called in the hundred leading students of the University and looked on while I showed them how to teach the Tagalog chart. "I am going home tonight," said President Bocobo, "and teach our cook. I challenge these students to make somebody literate before I do." He said he was trying to put a bill through the legislature to provide for a department of adult literacy.

Dr. Bocobo, Representative Fabian de la Paz, and Dean Francisco Benitez took me to see Governor-General Roosevelt, who had been keeping in touch with our progress ever since he had visited Lanao. The Governor-General said he had heard the fear expressed that our campaign would be used as Protestant propaganda. I replied that the only way to meet the objection was to take the movement out of missionary hands.

"At present," I told Mr. Roosevelt, "there is no government committee, and no non-religious committee of any kind, to which people can turn for information and literacy lessons. We have already set up five campaigns with municipal *presidentes* as their heads. For all their lesson material they must write to the National Christian Council, a Protestant organization. In Bangued the priest sent his principal teacher to learn our method. He must buy charts from the National Christian Council. Scores of high schools are taking up this cause with enthusiasm. They must write to the National Christian Council. Either the legislature or yourself should create a non-sectarian committee to study, stimulate, counsel, and coordinate the agencies interested in literacy and to furnish them books. I am sure that the Roman Catholic churches will cooperate with such a committee."

At the suggestion of the Governor-General, the Philippine Education Company agreed to print and sell packets containing the necessary teaching material. We devoted several days to writing instructions for teachers and organizers in seven dialects.

Governor-General Roosevelt also sent me to see Dr. Luther Bewley, Director of Education. "We have started literacy campaigns in ten of your high schools," I told him. "If all your high school and intermediate students will learn this method and teach their parents, they can wipe illiteracy out of this nation."

"You are right," Dr. Bewley replied, "but it takes time to get a huge organization like ours to undertake such a tremendous task. Meanwhile I hope you will visit all the schools in the Philippines."

When I reached San José, Antique, on the island of Panay—the last stop in my two months' tour—the Reverend E. F. Rounds took me to visit his friend, the Dutch priest. The padre was extremely cordial, offered us his best wine and cigars, and took us to see the eight Catholic sisters in the convent. These nuns, six of them Spanish and two of them Filipina, were lovely, spiritual women with a deep eagerness to help the illiterates who, they said, were very numerous in the province of Antique. For two hours they studied our charts and methods with keen interest.

As I traveled toward Lanao once more I listed the languages in which we had prepared key-word lessons. I counted twenty-one:

Maranaw	Ilocano	Joloano
Cebuan	Ibanag	Subano
Ilongo	Manobo	Bukidnon
Tagalog	Isinay	Bontoc Igorot
Bicol	Gaddang	Ifugao
Pampangan	Samarino	Kalinga
Pangasinan	Magindanao	Visayan

LITERACY SPREADS THROUGH THE ISLANDS

This was the beginning of the Philippine literacy campaigns. "But," you will ask, "did they continue?" Indeed they did and for this the National Christian Council deserves much of the credit. It appointed Miss Maria Dayoan general director of literacy in 1935, and until she came to America in 1938 she had astonishing results. At one of her early demonstrations before a huge crowd at the Philippines Normal School, the leading teachers' institution of the Islands, the illiterates learned to read so quickly that the crowd again and again broke into applause, and every student and teacher volunteered to teach. The Federation of Women's Clubs, one of the most powerful organizations in the Philippines, sent Miss Dayoan everywhere to train their leaders.

Her reports are full of happy experiences:

As I discovered how quickly people learned, I became more and more enthusiastic about literacy and was able to convince other people because of my own personal experience. Illiterates were taught far more rapidly than I had ever believed could be possible. In one demonstration before public school teachers, a woman was taught to read in twenty-five minutes. She was very much pleased and went home full of delight to tell her neighbors. Not long after she left, people flocked into the building. Many wanted to learn how to read and write, and others wanted to know how to teach their brothers, sisters, parents, or other relatives.

I have explained literacy and have trained teachers, not only in churches and women's clubs but also in parent-teacher associations, community assemblies, public and private schools, colleges, secondary and elementary schools, in lodges, municipal councils, dormitories, and student centers. The fact that I was representing the Federation of Women's Clubs enabled me to work with all sorts of organizations, with both Roman Catholic and Protestant groups as well as with those connected with no church.[1]

The Moros themselves were becoming deeply concerned with the progress of their people, and soon after

[1] From the *National Christian Council Bulletin*, April, 1936.

the first Independence Act was passed by Congress in 1932
I wrote of the hopes it had aroused:

January 27, 1933

I wish you could have been with me the other night as
our head printer, Macaindeg, poured out his passionate
longing to save his people. The passing of the Independence Bill by Congress is having a profound influence
upon these young Moros. They know that their province
is behind the rest of the Philippine Islands. Macaindeg
realizes that unless the Moros put forth a tremendous effort
to lift themselves educationally and economically during
the next ten years, they will be ruined when independence comes.

«««»»»

Meanwhile, the Governor-General took first steps toward a government department of adult education by
instituting a series of community assemblies. Over a hundred lectures on vital topics were sent throughout the
Islands to be delivered in all important languages.

Just as soon as the Philippines became a commonwealth,
the National Supreme Council established a Division of
Adult Education. This important development in the
progress of literacy took place in 1936. Thereafter, the
literacy campaign became a government enterprise and
reached out to every province and village. Literacy wagons
were sent over the Islands to attract all the illiterate adults
and give them reading lessons. Adult night schools were
established nearly everywhere.

The March, 1940, number of the government publication called *Adult Education* announced that the prize for the greatest number of illiterates taught to read that month had gone to the Davao Penal Colony. "The prisons," it said, "are becoming universities."

Matias Cuadra eventually became a chaplain in the Philippine army, and because of his experience in Lanao was given full charge of the literacy campaign among the armed forces. He pushed the campaign with such vigor that the army was nearly one hundred per cent literate when Japan struck.

A WORKING PARTNERSHIP

No account of our Lanao mission would be complete without a tribute to the magnificent men and women who worked with us during those years. They had come to the Philippines for sheer love of Christ and the romance of this great literacy adventure.

First, in 1930, came Mrs. David Lund, who opened our Moro girls' dormitory, paying her own salary and contributing fifty dollars a month to aid poor Moro girls. Mrs. Laubach came in 1931 to teach Moro women and keep our books, and with her came our thirteen year old son Bob and the Reverend and Mrs. Irving M. Channon, for years missionaries in the Caroline Islands and later at Silliman University, situated on Negros Island within sight of Mindanao. They gave us an extra year before retiring. Irving Channon could do more things than any other man I ever knew. With the aid of our Japanese neighbor, Mr. Matsui, he actually built us a home.

Late in 1931 the Woodwards, in whose home I had stayed on my first visit to Mindanao, moved to Lanao so that, while Mr. Woodward continued his evangelistic work along the coast of the island, his wife could help in the huge task of building a dictionary and translating the Bible.

In the summer of 1932 I was overjoyed to receive a letter from Miss Minnie K. Schultz in Pennsylvania, whose interest had been aroused by the magazine articles she had read about our literacy campaign and who wanted to come out to help us. Friends in America contributed funds to cover her salary, and in January of the following year she arrived to act as secretary and librarian. She won our hearts by her splendid spirit and by the intelligence with which she grasped the work. She was the first person of our acquaintance to go out and secure her own salary before starting out into the field—a wonderful thing to accomplish during those years of depression.

Mrs. Pearl Spencer, one of the famous early government teachers—"best principal in the Philippines," the Director of Education told me—also joined our mission group for educational work at one-sixth of her previous salary. In 1941 she became the first head of our Moro High School.

In 1940 the American Board of Commissioners for Foreign Missions sent us the Reverend Alvin H. Scaff and his wife, both of them members of Phi Beta Kappa; and in the fall of 1941, when the situation in Japan grew tense and the Japanese Christian leaders urged the missionaries to leave, the Reverend Darley Downs came to our Lanao station. When the tragic war struck the Philippines, Darley Downs, Marion Woodward, and Pearl Spencer were still in Lanao, all three of them separated from their families, who happened to be in the United States. All of them are marvelous Christians, warm friends of the Japanese, Chinese, and Filipinos as well as of the Moros, and we know that their influence is still felt as they continue to give witness to the love of Christ in Lanao.

While our mission force was thus growing, there was coming over the Moros a change so profound that it was nothing less than miraculous. When we arrived in 1929 the atmosphere was tense with hatred between the Moros and the constabulary. The government was trying to "keep the boat from rocking" as much as possible. Everybody except the missionaries carried guns—even in the daylight in the military camps—in 1929. But in thirteen years this had nearly all disappeared. And in 1942 these same Moros who had so hated us signed a solemn pledge that they would die rather than allow the Japanese to overthrow the good government established by the United States. Ten thousand Moros signed their names to this pledge— most of them men whom we had taught to read. They had stopped glorying in being outlaws and were proud of being good citizens. Fourteen years ago they had burned fifty school buildings, determined to root education out of Lanao. In 1941 we left them clamoring for schools faster than the government could provide them, and sending girls as well as boys to be educated.

At the time of the Japanese invasion we still had the

only press printing Maranaw literature. We were producing close to a million pages a year, although it had to be set up by hand or mimeographed. In the ten-year period preceding we had published booklets with stories of the Old Testament prophets, running both the Bible and Koran accounts in the same volume. We had printed *Luke* in Maranaw; and when the war broke out the American Bible Society was in the process of printing *Acts*. We had printed three editions of an English-Maranaw dictionary, with definitions of ten thousand words. And we were issuing *Lanao Progress*, a sixteen-page fortnightly.

We had specialized in paper-bound booklets and pamphlets, which we sold and gave away by tens of thousands. The non-religious pamphlets were on such varied subjects as "Care of the Skin," "Motherhood and Baby Care," "The New Miracle Rice," "Moro Folklore in Prose," and "History of the World." The Bureau of Education took the entire edition of a hundred-page volume containing a compilation of Moro lyrics. The religious pamphlets besides the Bible were on such themes as "Life on Its Highest Levels," "Three Hundred Objectives of Character," "God Is Beyond Us All," "Why Does God Permit Suffering?," "Where Christians and Moslems are Brothers," "Secrets of a Student's Success," "Game with Minutes" (now published in America), and a series of sixty four-page tracts on "The Friendship of Jesus" for distribution in the Moro markets.[1]

[1] In 1942 published by Harper & Brothers, New York, in book form under the title *You Are My Friends*.

LOVE THEM INTO LEARNING

During all these adventures we were developing a science and technique in adult literacy that we believed would be distinct contributions to education. This was in part the art of building easy lessons, to be sure, but it was far more than that—more than anything that could be written on paper. It was a thing of the spirit—the art of applying to education that mysterious love power that held together the early followers of Jesus.

Experience has shown us that it is necessary to produce a congenial spiritual climate if a campaign is to flourish. So the training of teachers involves far more than teaching them to say the right words. It is helping them to be warm friends of their students, to pray for them, to rejoice in their progress—in a word, to radiate a Christlike atmosphere.

One day after I had taught a half-dozen women and children to read while fifty teachers looked on, the chairman rose and said, "I have watched this remarkable exhibition and I believe I have found the secret. It is love." He was at least fifty per cent right. The psychological principles that we explain to all our teachers are the "highest" secret, not only of the literacy enterprise described in this book, but of life.

We prefer to teach one by one so that we may sit down beside our students; a teacher of a class is too much like a superior person. Every illiterate has an inferiority complex—he thinks we feel above him. The very first thing is to remove the gap between us. When we sit beside him we disarm his feeling of inferiority. Then we proceed to treat him not like a student but like a rajah! We try to make ourselves humble and him important. He thinks he is too old to learn. We must prove that he can learn easily, quickly, and delightfully, no matter how old he is. Every step is so short that an ordinary man can take it easily. The chart provides for this; but occasionally the teacher must say just the right word to help a dull student over a hard spot. There must be no embarrassing pauses, never a question the student cannot answer, no examination to find out what he knows!

We must keep out of the student's way, neither pushing him nor retarding him. An illiterate is happy only when he feels free to take his own natural gait.

On every line of the chart the student finds himself saying something surprising. An atmosphere of expectancy is thus developed; we can see it in the bright, open-mouthed eagerness of our illiterate learner. The chart becomes a Pandora's box of glad surprises, appealing to the emotions and drawing forth peals of laughter.

There is never a frown nor a rebuke nor a loud tone of voice. Students remember a whisper better than a howl because it is pleasanter. In teaching an illiterate there must be no unpleasant moments. Never a gesture of impatience nor a yawn. Upon the slightest justification we pat him on the shoulder and say, "That's fine." The student strives to maintain this charmed spell, perhaps the most thrilling hour of his life! He is getting along much better than he had expected because the lesson is easy and we teach correctly. He attributes it to his brilliance. What everybody craves, of all things on earth, is to have some hidden genius discovered in him. If you become the discoverer of that genius, he is yours, body and soul.

We have seen hundreds of men and women going out from their first lessons wreathed in smiles, saying, "Very easy! He was surprised at my bright mind." And after that all the others in the village are eager to have their brilliance discovered! We never forget that while we are teaching one man we are selling the idea to his neighbors.

Then, when the student has learned Lesson One, we set him to teaching somebody else. We look delighted at his teaching and say when he finishes, "You are going to be a splendid teacher. Teach about five more as you did now. Then I'll give you the next lesson." His teaching others has these obvious advantages:

1. The lesson is well fixed in his mind by the time he has taught it five or six times. We never really know a thing until we have used it.

2. He is at once given a new status in society, a new self-respect. He becomes a member of the teaching profession. It is astounding how his shoulders go back, his face beams, his eyes gleam—he has arrived!

3. By making every student a teacher, the teaching is done at small cost, and the increase in readers is very rapid. We educate by geometrical progression.

4. Our student comes to realize that he is learning in order to help others. The spirit of sharing is fostered.

Nothing I have ever seen begets friendship so effectively

as thus teaching illiterates and sending them out to teach others; not even a doctor, caring for the sick, has quite the same chance. For while the doctor and nurse do something *for the patient*, they do not request him to *go and cure others*. On the other hand, when we teach we ask our student to pass it on. He goes out with the feeling that he has surprised us, and that now we expect big things of him. Warm with gratitude, he tries to merit our further praise, and there is established a bond of affection that will last a lifetime. The student emulates our warm kindliness, so that it begins to permeate the entire community like some beneficent contagion. The spirit of sharing is taught, not by talking about it, but by doing it, and—what is even more vital—recruiting others to do it.

CHAPTER FOUR

A Literacy Tour across Southern Asia

OUR Moro teachers kept asking, "Do you suppose we can really make lessons as easy as these in other languages?" We knew it could not be done in English with its hopeless spelling. But what we were all eager to know was how many of the languages of the world were spelled regularly enough to be taught by our method.

Matias Cuadra, our Moro preacher, had lived in Borneo for several years and fortunately spoke Malay. He went to work preparing lessons in our front schoolroom while a hundred Moros looked on with mouths agape. In two days he had a Malay chart completed and the whole Moro tribe clamored to read it, for they think Malay is nearly as sacred as Arabic. Cuadra almost became their god. Having tasted that triumph, we were all eager for more.

Many missionaries wrote us from India, men who had beaten their heads against the stone wall of illiteracy for twenty or thirty years. These men asked us to visit them, though one of them warned us to expect "a task about equal to shoveling the Himalayas into the Indian Ocean." "We shall never have a strong indigenous church in India," he wrote, "until more of its members can read the Scriptures; and so I am keenly interested. Even though I fear that your visit will be a disappointment to you in the way of definite results, I do believe you will stir up interest in the subject."

It was our irrepressibly enthusiastic secretary, Minnie Schultz, who really pushed us over the brink into world literacy tours. She persuaded me to prepare a letter for persons along our route to America via India and Suez, which we would be taking when we left on furlough. Before I realized it Miss Schultz had mimeographed and mailed five hundred copies of this letter! Many of those who received it sent us most urgent invitations to visit them.

We wrote accepting invitations from Singapore, Ceylon, parts of India, Cairo, Palestine, Syria, and Turkey, and on January 20, 1935, I set out alone, half frightened at my own audacity! We had no resources except a furlough travel allowance, so, to save expenses, Mrs. Laubach, our son Bob, and Miss Schultz remained in Lanao two months longer and met me in Colombo after I had finished my visit in India.

FAREWELL TO MOROLAND

On shipboard from Lanao to Manila I wrote to my father telling him all about the farewell celebrations the Moros had held for us:

January 20, 1935

At last I am on the way home. What a farewell we had! For days we had felt excitement in the air as we packed our baggage to leave, but we did not expect a *despedida* as overwhelming as those dear Moros gave us.

Five big trucks filled with them followed our car down to Iligan, the seaport twenty-five miles away. They swarmed on the ship and spilled over on the wharf. Every high *dato* in Lanao wanted to make a speech on how they were sending me to bring light to mankind and how this was to be the beginning of emancipation for the human race, the turning point in world history! At ten that night the captain blew his whistle to warn that he was about to cast off, but the Moros laughed and went on talking. The captain subsided for fear they would cut his head off. When every *dato* had made his speech the sheik said: "We are going to pray for you." They could not bow to the deck for they were crowded together like sardines, so they held out their hands and kept turning them over, palms up, palms down, while their highest *imam* prayed that this American friend, whom they had helped to make the easiest lessons in the world, should have the blessing of Allah as he went around the world introducing their method to the less fortunate nations. Then they kissed me and hugged me and one-eyed Hadji Kakairan cried on my shoulder as he said: "We will pray for you in every mosque in Lanao while you go around the world spreading the glory of Lanao." They declared they would have gone along if only they could have sold their brass pots for cash! A dozen Moros did go as far as Manila.

«««»»»

When later I told the Moslems in Malacca, India, Palestine, Syria, Dar es Salaam, and Zanzibar that these Moslem friends in Lanao were praying for us, they laughed with delight and hugged me as only Moslems hug brothers. When anybody tells me that it is hard to make friends among Moslems I know better. They do get angry when we throw stones at their religion, but who can blame them when we ourselves are so horribly unlike our Christ? I have found among Moslems as loyal and true friends as among any Christians in the world, and some Moslems, especially the Sufis, are truly saints.

The expectancy with which Christians and Moslems received us across southern Asia was not only astonishing, it was embarrassing! We were thrown at once into the limelight, although we were still timid explorers and our methods were in the experimental stage, changing from one week to the next. So greatly did people feel the need of literacy help that they wanted to believe we were infallible.

BEGINNINGS IN MALAYA

The first place I touched was Singapore. The missionaries told me that the Malay language is not much used in that city, which is largely made up of Chinese, Indians, and whites, so they packed me off to Malacca, a hundred miles to the north. The Reverend and Mrs. Robert A. Blaisdell collected a dozen Moslem boys in a few minutes, and since I had only two days to work before returning to Singapore to catch the boat, we toiled with feverish haste, day and night, taking out an hour for church, until Sunday noon. We were still working while we ate our last meal together, papers in hand, and were past the hardest points when I ran to catch the mail car. Later the Blaisdells sent me a beautiful set of Malay lessons exactly like those in the Philippines, and just as easy, for Malay belongs to the same language family and has many of the same words.

Three years afterward one of the leaders in Singapore wrote:

We are going ahead in Malay with the method of teaching illiterates that you worked out with Mr. and Mrs. Blaisdell. There are great possibilities here, for the statistics show that only twenty-five per cent of the people are literate, and in the village districts and the jungle not ten per cent can read.

One difficulty is the fact that all Malay education is officially in the hands of the British Department of Education, which is naturally a bit nervous about a mission crashing into a field where they have had the monopoly. Moreover, the government is afraid we may use literacy as an entering wedge for Christian missions among the Malays.

«««»»»

Of course literacy is an opening wedge for any idea or movement, good or bad, among a backward people. But the British fear that it might start a wave of religious fanaticism in Malaya was groundless. Our experience in Mindanao had demonstrated that a literacy campaign, far from causing unrest, was the best possible way to bring loyal cooperation.

We found another curious complication at Singapore. The British spell the Malay language the English way, and the Dutch in Sumatra, within sight of Singapore, spell it the Dutch way! So whenever Malays in British territory desire to write to Malays in Dutch Sumatra, they have to use Arabic letters because the English and Dutch spellings are so far apart. I told the Inspector of Schools in Singapore that I thought this was ridiculous, and he replied, "Oh, not at all, not at all! Variety is the spice of life, don't you know? It would be a pity to have the monotony of spelling Malay only one way." Now, I suppose, they are spelling it the Japanese way, which will still further relieve the monotony.

A FIRST ATTEMPT IN HINDI

On the steamer from Singapore to India was an Indian, Mr. G. D. Mehrottra, who became very keen to help make Hindi lessons without waiting to reach Bombay. Another passenger, Miss Caroline Pope, who was a missionary from India, caught Mehrottra's enthusiasm. Using her Hindi dictionary we three labored and wrestled every day to find key words—or rather they labored and I wrestled.

The very first day it became evident that we could not make lessons as easy as those we had made in the Philippines because the Hindi alphabet was far more complicated. In Lanao we had sixteen letters, but Hindi had fifty.

Moreover, they have the split and spliced letters, half of one letter on top of half another. The reason for this is that every consonant has a vowel sound understood. We went through the dictionary twice and could not find good key words for all their consonants—they just did not exist.

"Mehrottra," I said, "I'm going to cable my wife to come on the next ship and sail right on past India. I'm licked."

But Mehrottra never lost his courage. "This," he said, "is what India needs most of all. Our people are ninety per cent illiterate, and somebody has got to help us out. Let's try again. Put the letters that sound alike in families, then we can find key words. Let's put 'p' and 'b' in one family, 't' and 'd' in another, and so on."

We tried that and had fifteen families and five beautiful key words in half an hour! By the time we reached Bombay we had finished the first set of key-word lessons ever made in an Indian language. We walked down the gangplank into India feeling like Hannibal plunging out of the Alps into Italy on his elephant. Little did I dream what Himalayas lay ahead! It is providential that they were hidden from my eyes. India had known them too well and they had defeated her so long that she was deep in a slough of despond. She needed easier lessons, it is true, but even more she needed new faith. As I took the train from Bombay to Nagpur to meet the National Christian Council, I rashly supposed that I had one answer to India's problems already tucked under my arm.

The evening I arrived in Nagpur, Mahatma Gandhi was dining with the secretary of the National Christian Council, Dr. J. Z. Hodge, who arranged for me to call upon the Mahatma at Wardha the following week. We had nothing to show Mr. Gandhi, so we had to work fast. Three Indian women and one man, all of them teachers, poured themselves with intense enthusiasm for six days into preparing Marathi charts in colors to lay before their famous leader.

At his little house in Wardha, Mr. Gandhi received me courteously, but, like all the other leaders at the time, he despaired of making India literate so long as she was hungry and destitute. Our conversation on this occasion has been briefly reported in the first chapter. As we drove home that evening my British companion said, "Gandhi thinks you are attempting the impossible." "Fools rush in where angels fear to tread," I replied and we both laughed. If you can't laugh at yourself, don't set out to reform the world.

One of the tricks a traveler in India has to learn is to provide his own bedding in winter. The inexperienced newcomer on his first journey is likely to get into a train that is stifling hot at five o'clock in the evening, without blankets or overcoat, and then wake up at midnight with teeth chattering. I took a night train from Nagpur without enough blankets and long before daybreak tumbled out of my bunk shivering, wishing I were in Lanao and tempted to blame God for getting me into this "fix."

At the station at Raipur a man in shorts walked up and said, "My name is Moyer. Is your name Laubach?"

"Moyer! Why, I thought you lived a hundred miles from here."

"I do," said Moyer, "but I just drove in to meet you and take you on down to Dhamtari."

"And you got here at four A. M.! Did you get any sleep?"

"Yes, plenty. I slept on the station benches."

I put my arm around him and said, "Man, you make me weep. If you hadn't been here, I would have taken the next train right back to Bombay. I'm scared about your expectations."

"Never mind," said Moyer. "We are all praying, and God wants this done more than anybody else. You'll win."

That is the way the missionaries were all over India; there is no more wonderful group of Christians on this planet. But then, I've felt the same way about the missionaries in every country I ever visited!

Dhamtari is on the edge of an Indian jungle, where the tigers love to lie across the road at night and worry belated auto drivers. Every missionary has seen them. The big cats look into the headlights, stretch, move lazily off the road, and try to peer into the windows while the cars pass, but they have never struck a car yet. Americans at this Mennonite mission at Dhamtari, together with their Indian colleagues, worked on the Hindi lessons for a month, and each evening we all went to a near-by village of outcastes to try out our lessons on illiterate leather workers, the Chamars. The lessons worked well on them, so we tried them at a camp of three hundred lepers, and then had them printed. The Reverend J. D. Graber took over the supervision of these experimental lessons and improved them until they were really good.

INTO THE SOUTH

The following month I went with Dr. Mason Olcott, of the Union Teachers' Training School near Katpadi, and about sixteen of his teachers into another remote region a hundred miles northwest of Madras, where Dr. Olcott worked with eight teachers on Tamil lessons and the other eight teachers worked on Telugu. I acted as the guinea pig on which both groups tried their lessons. Tamils can say longer words and say them faster than any other people on earth—like a muffled rapid-fire gun. It is spoken by more than twenty million people. Telugu, used by upwards of twenty-six millions, is a lovely language, often called the "Italian of India." We went out every evening to a Tamil or Telugu mud village to experiment, and had illiterates teaching one another as far as the rays of our powerful Mazda lantern would reach. We all slept in a hot schoolroom. It was cooler outside, but panthers lived in the near-by rocks.

The third week we became a three-ring circus. The headmaster of the Moslem Government School of Vellore brought his staff of teachers to our country schoolhouse to make Urdu lessons, but they shouted and argued so zealously that the Tamil and Telugu gangs had to move off thirty yards to hear themselves talk.

The president of the Arabic College in Madras took me home with him, gathered the Moslem leaders to his college in a great meeting, staged a successful demonstration of our method, put wreaths of fragrant flowers around my neck, and made such speeches as I had never heard before.

At the lovely summer residence center of Kodaikanal, seven thousand feet above the sea, a hundred deeply interested missionaries met me one afternoon for a demonstration of the Tamil charts. As we closed, one of the men took my hand and said with deep feeling, "If I had a million dollars, I would give it to you for this work in India!" That is exactly what somebody ought to do for literacy in India— give it a million dollars.

Those missionaries ordered five thousand sets of Tamil and Telugu lessons, sight unseen. When I left them I was weak and frightened. The lessons were very rough and imperfect; they would need long months or years of patient improvement to be very successful. I had told everybody this. But would they believe it, or would they cast them aside at the first trouble? It was with those misgivings and with my task hardly begun that I turned my back on India. People would be trying these first hastily prepared lessons in Hindi, Marathi, Telugu, Tamil, and Urdu—would they, I wondered, ever want to see me again?

ADVENTURE IN ARABIC

I met Mrs. Laubach, Bob, and Miss Schultz at Colombo and together we sailed on to Cairo, where there awaited us one of the most surprising welcomes we have ever had. This, too, was connected with Signal Hill, and it was God pushing me into deep water! Here is what happened.

A friend in New York had kept a scrapbook of letters to my father as they came out each week in the Benton *Argus*. He had sent them the previous year to Miss Constance

Padwick, secretary of the Central Literature Committee for Moslems in Cairo. Miss Padwick had mimeographed selections from those letters and sent them to missionaries and Christian workers throughout the Near East.[1] So when we reached Cairo, they hurried me off to a Near East Christian conference timed especially for the occasion, and everybody treated me like a long-lost brother. The Egyptians greeted me in Oriental fashion and said, "We have read about you and your Moro friends. Do the same thing for us in Egypt that you did for them."

Forty missionaries and nationals volunteered to take turns in shifts of ten each to prepare Arabic lessons. Miss Padwick had a book called *Phonetics of Arabic*, which arranged the letters into families exactly as we had been doing in India. We took this arrangement to our committee and asked them to find key words. In all my life I have never seen such brilliant work. They found three key words in ten minutes! The committee then made lessons with such wit and skill and joy that people couldn't wait for their shift—they did not want to miss the fun. In two days we had completed five charts. The press mimeographed thirty copies each of all five lessons, so that people could experiment with them.

All that week I had no time for sightseeing—only one swift look at the pyramids by moonlight. Miss Padwick and our family ate supper in the dusk under the ghostly

---

[1] These have now been printed in the United States under the title *Letters by a Modern Mystic* (New York, Student Volunteer Movement, 1937).

shadows of the oldest pyramid in the world. The air seemed full of the spirits of millions of those slaves who had toiled in that sand five thousand years ago. We were told that they had piled up the sand and dragged the stones to the very top of that lofty pyramid and then had dug all the sand away again, leaving the most stupendous mass of masonry on earth towering above the desert.

The doctor in the hospital in Old Cairo invited us to try our new charts on his convalescent patients. Forty missionaries and Egyptians gathered to see the experiment. The hospital doctor brought in thirty illiterate convalescents, and each member of the audience was given one illiterate to teach for twenty-five minutes.

They returned with grave faces, and Miss Padwick's face looked as sick as my heart felt. I realized that I had made a major mistake in allowing all those forty people to teach instead of teaching them how to do it first. And I should have tested the students' eyes first. For the doctor arose and informed us that every convalescent in his hospital had eye disease, and probably could not see the letters anyhow! What did he think we had—a Braille system? Everybody laughed, but the beans had been spilled. The whole over-expectant gathering had hoped for a miracle and an easy victory. They did not realize that persistence is our only secret; that months, perhaps years, of hard work with the Arabic language would be necessary before we could claim success.

One of the chief advantages of traveling from region to region is that when one committee is worn to a frazzle or becomes discouraged, you find the next group fresh and eager to begin. And you never breathe a word about your last troubles. For an inner voice tells you it is not defeat, only delay.

At Jerusalem the principal of the Newman School of Missions invited fifty missionaries and Palestinians, some of them members of the Bureau of Education, to a meeting the first afternoon we arrived. This was followed by nine more addresses that week—and in between we revised the lessons that had just been made in Cairo.

I showed them to the British Director of Education and eight of his staff. Some of the Palestinians did not like the words we had used, said they were not classical words. A hot debate broke out as to whether colloquial words ought ever to be used. I was horrified. "Of course," I told them, "people must learn to read familiar words first, before they attempt unknown words." "No, no, no, no!" the pundits objected. "Our scholars would never tolerate such degradation of literature!" There in the Holy City I had my first battle with the fastidious scholar who would have classical words or none, no matter whether illiterates learned to read or not. This stupid mistake, I learned later, was Asia's worst foe to literacy. They ended the debate by deciding to try to prepare a list of all the classical words the illiterates used in conversation—if there were any—and use these "pure" but well known words in building lessons.

The next day the two leading primary school specialists of Palestine were sent by the Director of Education to Ain Karim, the birthplace of John the Baptist, five miles west of Jerusalem, to experiment with me on illiterate Moslems. One of them, Mr. Hannosh, taught the first boy, he the second, the second the third; all of them behaved brilliantly. To my deep delight, Constance Padwick arrived in the very middle of the experiment. She had come all the way from Cairo "to see whether we were yet killing the giant illiteracy." Her cheeks flushed with pleasure as she saw the giant at least dealt a severe blow under the chin. And I breathed a prayer of thanksgiving for her sake.

My family tarried another week to see Jerusalem while I hurried on to Beirut to make more charts. I was in such a frenzy to make those Arabic charts better that I felt few regrets at missing the most wonderful land in the world for any Christian to visit. The Jerusalem experiment had been an improvement over the Cairo failure, but already my head was buzzing with new ideas, and I needed a fresh committee on which to try them.

On the way I went to visit the ruins of Capernaum alone, and stood a long while in the very synagogue where Jesus had taught and outside whose doors he had cured so many sick. I could not help repeating over and over, "Master, you really stepped here and sat here as you spoke," and I caressed the stones as I fairly felt him walking there unseen again.

My stay in Beirut was nothing short of breathless— twenty-five different addresses during six days. Such excellent plans had been made by friends in the American University and the Near East School of Theology that we also found time for rebuilding the Arabic lessons. There were only two members in my committee, but they were a joy. Professor Tannus was a Syrian in the American University. Miss Nejla Izzadin, Ph.D., a graduate of Vassar College with her doctorate from the University of Chicago, was a Druse. My notes say: "She eats original research of this kind as though it were chocolate candy."

No doubt the keen interest of Dr. Izzadin was due to her desire for her own people, the Druses, to become literate. They are a strange, proud, wonderful race of people, who believe themselves to be superior, never changing their religious convictions, and never intermarrying with outsiders. Miss Izzadin, with all her travels and education, seemed as much a Druse as ever. We could not complete the charts before I was compelled to leave, but those two Syrian scholars finished and printed them after I was gone—the best Arabic lessons for adults ever made. That summer Miss Izzadin and a camp of students from the Junior College in Beirut taught the illiterates in some Syrian villages. This is what she wrote me about that experience:

This may mean much to Syria, ninety per cent of whose population is still illiterate. Cordially and enthusiastically the Nusaireyeh villagers welcomed us; the women wanted to know when the children were to be taught—but having the adults learn to read was too entirely unheard of! Had they not existed all these years without knowing how to read and write? Why trouble themselves now? Even Sheik Ali shook his head. "No, some are born to be educated like the sheiks, and others must work and till the soil.

What respect would the workers have for us, if they, too, could read?"

Grudgingly permission was given that the older girls and women might come, but these, long used to being told that they were too stupid to learn, said they dared not leave their work. Nevertheless, three came, more from curiosity than interest, and, pleased with their rapid progress, brought three others the second day, and twenty the third! Possibly the unexpected opposition was the best way to get the movement going, for Sheik Ali has now sent word that next week his whole village will be ready to start.

《《《》》》

Every summer since that student camps from Beirut have carried on campaigns among the illiterate villagers of Syria.

While I was in Beirut Mr. Uwum Seadat published an article that is loaded with truth:

Dr. Laubach's lectures and illustrations fill me with great hopes and they also arouse in me great fears. I am afraid that here is another blessing that God has bestowed upon the world that will be used for evil ends.

To teach the Syrians to read and write means to release a great new power in Syria. But for what? So that Syria may advance in the direction in which it is moving at the present time? It is hardly worth the effort. It seems to me that we need to set our goal first. What can be done to bridge the tremendous gap that exists and is widening between Christians and Moslems, or what can we do about the great hatred that the Arabs have for the Jews? Can we utilize this great new power of literacy to bridge those gaps?

Unless persons with a spiritual motive take hold of it and further it for specific spiritual ends, the whole movement will be a curse. People who have experienced love, sacrifice, and service must take this great task upon their shoulders.

What Uwum Seadat said about Syria applies to all Asia and Africa—and the world.

THE NEW TURKEY

Turkey is changing with incredible rapidity, like her neighbor Russia. A republic in form, Turkey became in reality a dictatorship under President Mustafa Kemal—Kemal Ataturk, as he chose in 1934 to be called ("Ataturk" means "Father of the Turks"). He was a highly efficient dictator with good ideas and enormous capacity to get things done. In 1928 he threw Arabic out of the schools and replaced it with a splendid Latin phonetic alphabet. It all happened during the summer vacation period. No textbooks with the old script were permitted in the schools when they reopened that fall. The children had to start all over like first graders with these unknown letters. No religious teaching was permitted in the school programs because Kemal Ataturk believed the Moslem priests were obstructing education. John Dewey and other well known educators were asked to come and introduce the latest educational ideas. Turkish teachers were sent abroad to glean the world's best ideas. All education became free and compulsory.

Night schools for adults were opened everywhere. Kemal Ataturk himself became a teacher to set the educated people an example. The government announced that jobs would go only to those who could read and write. In four years two millions were taught. The coffee houses began to lose business and the seventeen hundred libraries of the country were crowded.

The atmosphere in Turkey in 1935 was unlike any we have ever experienced. One could fairly feel the iron hand of Kemal Ataturk as he crashed through old customs to achieve his idea of progress. He had been breaking the power of the Moslem church leaders by one edict after another, (even compelling priests to read the Koran in Turkish instead of in the sacred Arabic language.) While we were there the priests and nuns, Moslem as well as Christian, were forced to abandon clerical garb, to adopt Western costumes and cut their hair *à la Parisienne*. Dr. F. W. McCallum said one evening as we strolled through Istanbul, "Take your last look at the priests and nuns, for tomorrow you'll not see any." And we didn't! But we could spot the priests by the awkward way they wore Western trousers!

My old friend the Reverend John Kingsley Birge, with whom I had worked at Spring Street Neighborhood House in New York City in 1910, had been in Turkey for many years as a missionary. His most important contribution to the new Turkish education was a scientific word count to determine the one thousand "basic" Turkish words, the ones that would be needed in order to teach illiterates.

He counted words from five sources—government reports, conversation, school readers, village literature, and Turkish newspapers—and found these startling facts:

Four Turkish words make up *twelve per cent* of the word occurrences, one-eighth of all the words in the Turkish language.

Twenty-seven words make up *twenty-four per cent* of the word occurrences.

In the Turkish New Testament he found that

Fifty-eight words make up *thirty-three per cent* of the word occurrences.

Three hundred and three words make up *seventy per cent* of the word occurrences.

King Birge's first five hundred and first thousand most used Turkish words are now in use in the government primary schools.

Unfortunately Birge was out of Turkey on his furlough in 1935 when we paid our visit, but he had given me helpful introductions to government officials. Dr. Paul Monroe, then president of Robert College, also introduced me to important educational leaders.

The Director of Education, Husein Bey, asked me to make a set of lessons and submit them to his government. I was also invited in Ankara to the headquarters of the *Halk Evi* or People's party (the only political party they had in Turkey), which was responsible for adult literacy. They entertained me like the Shah of Persia, and told me one of the strangest stories that ever came to my ears. The Turkish leaders, they said, were feeding their people a new language in spoonfuls—five new words a day, which everybody must memorize. They were making the people believe that these words had been rescued from the ancient Hittite civilization from which, so they told the people, the modern Turks had descended. Hundreds of scientific words like "electricity," "radio," and "telegraph" did not come from Europe—perish the thought! They came from "our ancestors, the Hittites."

In Istanbul we found an excellent committee of scholars and in three days we had finished fifteen lessons by working many hours overtime every day. Just before our ship was to sail, we sent them off to the Director of Education. From Mindanao to Turkey we had built charts in thirty languages.

I shall never forget one member of that fine Turkish committee—a Persian by birth. He was blind and had to be led to our meetings by his daughter. He possessed such fine spiritual insight that I told him, "We are the blind ones and you alone can see into reality." He begged me to go to Iran, where, he told me, "not one person in a hundred can read." But I lacked time and—what I did not tell him—money. Indeed, this whole venture was coming out of a missionary's meager allowance. So we left on the last lap of our long journey to America before our pockets were empty.

CHAPTER FIVE

Around the World and Back to India

WHEREVER Americans heard the story of the world's enormous need for literacy, as I traveled over the country during my furlough year 1935-36, their response was always the same—they were stunned to learn that China and India together have over seven hundred millions of illiterates—more than one-third of the human race—and that of the whole world's population, the greater part are still illiterate.

In the autumn of 1935 a group of interested friends formed the World Literacy Committee, which afterwards became a committee of the Foreign Missions Conference of North America. Its work is now included in that of a representative committee on World Literacy and Christian Literature. Through this committee, funds were provided for further traveling in the interests of literacy and for the extension of the program that had been initiated by the earlier journeys through the Philippines, India, and other parts of Asia.

In the summer of 1936 I left the United States for the

Orient and on my way attended a Seminar on Pacific Education held at Honolulu. Three hundred leading educators in countries bordering on the Pacific were present. Mr. I. J. Brugmans, Director of Education in the Dutch East Indies, Mr. Georges A. Bernard, assistant to the Director of Public Instruction in Hanoi, French Indo-China, and all the other delegates from Pacific areas listened to the story of our Philippines experiment with eager interest and urged me to visit their countries. There was not now, to my knowledge, a country on earth that remained closed to this movement. The organizer of the Seminar, the late Professor Charles T. Loram of the Yale Graduate School, went on with me to study at first hand the progress of our literacy campaign in the Philippine Islands.

I had planned to stay in the Philippines only a few days and then push on as rapidly as possible to India, but I was delayed in Manila for two months. Before leaving the Islands in 1934, I had showed the University Press an unfinished manuscript of a biography of José Rizal, the greatest Filipino known to history. The Press now urged me strongly to remain in Manila long enough to complete this, and I spent wonderful days with Rizal's three sisters —old ladies of eighty-four, seventy-eight, and seventy-four —coaxing from them many anecdotes of their brother. By great concentration I was able to finish the manuscript, but before I could complete the reading of the proofs I had to take ship for India.

A FRESH START IN TAMIL AND TELUGU

When I finally reached my destination in November, I was distressed to find that my delay had disrupted a crowded and carefully planned program in southern India. They had closed some schools, they had brought people in for many miles, and I had failed to arrive.

All I could say in amazement was, "I never dreamed that anybody cared whether I came back or not." "Cared!" they replied. "Stanley Jones has gone all over India, demonstrating what you showed him at Kodaikanal and insisting that we must make every Christian literate with all possible speed."

Other things, too, made my cheeks burn. The Tamil chart that we had prepared in Dr. Olcott's country school, wrote Lloyd Lorbeer of Madura frankly, "has not really taken hold. It is cheap, but except for that merit, it offers no improvement over books and charts now in the field. Many of the words used in your chart are unknown here in Madura." Reading those words gave me cold chills. I felt especially sorry for Mason Olcott and other friends who had invested so much money and so much time on those charts, only to have them fail. Had I been attempting the impossible? Had Gandhi been right?

But splendid Mason Olcott, with his bulldog under-jaw, was as resolved as ever. He said it was true that the Tamil charts had not succeeded, but then never mind, why should we expect success in such a brief time? We had not begun to fight yet. We would find the trouble and rectify it. He brought two Indian teachers to his home and the four of us spent seven days in a huddle around a table looking for our mistakes. We found it all too true that many of the words in our lessons were unfamiliar to illiterates and, what was worse, several were Telugu words. As though you had put French or Latin words in English primers—like *non compos mentis*, for example, which is precisely what it would be!

How did this happen? We had prepared the lessons in the border region between the Tamil and the Telugu country where the illiterates understood both languages. It did not take us long to weed out the Telugu and make sure every word was familiar.

At our conference with missionaries and Indian Christians in Madras the next week, we met two Indians who had devoted their long lives to literacy. Mr. S. G. Daniel, a lovable saint of seventy years, a born teacher, had been teaching men, women, and children for forty-five years and had developed the most widely used primer in the Tamil language. We watched him teach, his low, mellow, slightly tremulous voice holding the illiterates like magic. He spent one hour telling them about the letter "ee"—which means "fly." An entire hour on one letter, and they have two hundred and forty-seven letter forms to learn in Tamil! But then nobody is in a hurry in South India—it is too warm for speed.

The other was Mrs. A. Devasahayam, a gray-haired woman with a radiant face. She, too, had spent many years of her life teaching the Tamil alphabet. Her scheme was to arrange the letters that were shaped nearly alike into families and teach about ten letters at a time, as though we were to group "p, b, d, g, h" because they look alike. To prove that it would work she taught some illiterates for us, and on the third day they all knew their letters and thought it was fun. By many years of practice Mrs. Devasahayam had streamlined her teaching so that not a word was wasted.

It was not mere accident that Mr. Daniel and Mrs. Devasahayam, the two who had worked harder than any other Indians to make Madras literate, were both Christians. It was from Christ that they had received their deep passionate love for unfortunates and their perseverance in the face of the "impossible."

Bezwada, in the heart of the Telugu-speaking region a hundred and fifty miles north of Madras, is one of the famous mass movement areas, where tens of thousands, especially from the depressed classes, are joining the church. Here the leaders reported that the Telugu lessons that we had made at Mason Olcott's school the year before had proved successful. They did not want us to discard the lessons but only to leave out the unfamiliar words. There were a hundred Anglican missionaries and Indians assembled for our all-day meetings, their minds alert to find ways of helping their thousands of converts to learn to read.

I went to the Lutheran College in Guntur with unusual eagerness because its president was Dr. Roy Strock, the man who more than any other person had influenced me in my pre-college days to become a Student Volunteer.

He had been a teacher at Perkiomen School near Philadelphia, had coached our football team during the week, and had held a mission study class in his own room on Sunday. It was not the heroism in the books that impressed us so much as the heroism of Roy Strock. He had lost one eye through an accident only a few months before, but this did not prevent him from playing high-grade tennis, nor volunteering to go to Africa as a missionary. The way he rose above his misfortune made me love him—and his cause. He finally was sent to India, where the same power to make good in spite of handicaps pushed him to the front until he became secretary for the National Christian Council of all India. And now I was being entertained by my boyhood hero in his own home!

Another heart-moving experience awaited me in Guntur. We were hard at work on the revision of Telugu lessons when in walked a woman of about thirty, who was introduced to me as Miss Grace Chapman. She had an unmistakable Australian accent. This is what she told that group while I went limp with amazement:

"I have been a missionary teaching Moslem women in their homes in Sholapur. When I read in various journals about the success of the literacy movement among the Moslems in Mindanao, I made up my mind to go to the Philippines and see what they were doing. As it was my furlough time, I returned home to Australia, intending later to go from there to Mindanao. It happened that the Bishop of Dornakal was also visiting Australia and he told me that Dr. Laubach was returning to India and had probably reached there by now. So I packed my belongings and came right back to India as fast as I could travel without taking my furlough. The millions of illiterates in India are more important than my vacation."

Through the following months Grace Chapman went from one end of India to the other, stimulating literacy efforts among the Christians, who were her first interest. She wanted the Bible used for the very first lessons—and this was sound practice among Christians, because they were more eager to read the Bible than any other one book. She had already prepared a very beautiful *Gospel Primer* with limited word lists and it had been translated into many languages. Before Miss Chapman's untimely death a year later, she had stirred all Christian India with her passionate crusade. When my soul needs new courage I think of dear Grace Chapman, who would rather see India literate than take a furlough in her home country. Her spirit broods over her beloved India, and I pray that her vision may be captured in this book.

At Guntur, and at other points on this tour of India, there were debates over "story method versus the key-word method." We always came out at the same place—it is the language that determines which method is best.

In the English language, where "o," for example, has as many sounds as the entire Moro alphabet, we get far less confused if we begin with words from the very first, teaching the children a few each day from a story like "The Little Red Hen," and postponing the sad news about our crazy spelling until several weeks later.

Phonetics do not help much since we never know how to pronounce an English word until somebody tells us, and then we are not sure he knows.

In Maranaw, on the other hand, where there is only one possible sound for a letter and where there are only sixteen letters, it is easy to teach the adults all their sounds the first day, and a skillful teacher can do it in one hour. After that, the Moros can pronounce nearly every word for themselves, and the teacher has little need of saying much. Many have taught themselves to read after the first session. This is "lightning literacy" indeed, as compared to the story method, if you have a perfectly phonetic alphabet, because you have to teach only twenty to forty sounds instead of a thousand words.

The question which we discussed at Guntur was whether Telugu was phonetic enough so that the key-word method would work—a very important question. If it would work, we could adopt the "each one teach one" idea, for anybody could spare a few hours to start students one by one so they could go on teaching themselves. But if the key-word method would not work, then students would have to be taught constantly for a year or two, and nobody would teach that long without being paid for it. There was room for a real difference of opinion. Some of our delegates at Guntur were from teachers' colleges in New York and Chicago. They said, "Argument will not prove this question. Let us try both ways for a year, and compare notes." This they did; a year later everyone voted for the key-word method.

The Telugu language is not only the pleasantest to hear but the most beautiful to look at in all India, with the graceful curves of figure skating. It could be a perfect alphabet, if only a few dozen irregularities were omitted. But when you suggest this to a scholar, he tells you, "There is a tremendous literature in Telugu that has been written on palm leaves through the past three thousand years." "A far greater literature," declared one pundit, "than you have in English. Who dares change this sacred writing for mere simplicity in learning!" The obvious answer is, "Nobody dares."

After the Guntur meeting Mr. K. G. Sundaram, principal of the teachers training school at Dornakal, prepared an excellent key-word primer in Telugu. He has since become one of the five or six great literacy leaders of India. Never discouraged and never satisfied, he has persisted in experiments with tireless tenacity, until he has developed a key-word adult primer as streamlined as a Cadillac.

Sundaram took me home with him to Dornakal, where I had two never-to-be-forgotten days at the home of Dr. Azariah, Bishop of Dornakal, one of those Anglican spiritual giants who remind one of the late great Bishop Brent. Azariah was black with the blazing sun of South India, but in every other respect like an English bishop, if anything more so! For years he has been recognized as the leader of Indian evangelical Christianity. It was amazing to see groups of Indians, all of them from the depressed classes, stopping the bishop along the road to ask whether they might not be received into his church.

INTO THE MARATHI COUNTRY

Another of the influential Christians of India is Professor Bhaskarao P. Hivale of Wilson College, Bombay. He received his Ph.D. degree from Harvard University and has had long periods of residence in America. Full of energy and optimism, it is natural that he should be made chairman of nearly everything. I saw him at his best as chairman of a retreat at Poona that December. Nationals and missionaries combined prayer, eager dedication of self to the stupendous task, and clear, efficient planning in a remarkable synthesis of vision and hard work. Lillian Picken's face fairly shone when she told us how she longed to open the most priceless of all books to her illiterate Indian Christians as she carried forward her reconstruction program at Satara, in Bombay Presidency.

We went from that retreat in an ecstasy like that of the Christians after Pentecost, to prepare lessons in Marathi—a language used by more than twenty millions of people. Twenty people had been at work for a week before I arrived and had already discovered key-words. To finish the task required only a few more days of delightful if strenuous application. Dr. Hivale was brilliant throughout. He wanted the lessons printed at once, even though they were still only the first rough draft. He argued that the swiftest way to experiment was to have a large number of persons trying the lessons simultaneously and pooling their experiences.

"Yes," I said, "if you do not kill the enthusiasm of the experimenters by that process."

"Never worry about us," he answered. "Nothing can kill our zeal, for this has got to be done."

I yielded to his infectious faith, and he printed five hundred copies at his own expense and gave them away to everybody who would experiment with them.

The following week he delivered a stirring inaugural speech as president of the All-India Conference of Indian Christians at Delhi, in which he declared: "We can make every Christian in India literate by 1941 if we adopt the motto 'Each one teach one' and go home to see that every literate Christian does his duty." Hivale's speech became the watchword for all Christian India. "Every literate Christian do his duty . . . Each one teach one . . . Indian Christians literate by 1941."

Christmas Eve, 1936, found me in a crowded third-class railway carriage alone among strangers. I might as well have been on Mars. Nobody, so far as I knew, was a Christian, and I could not ask them because I could not speak Marathi. Perhaps nobody else in that car even knew it was Christmas Eve! I was lonesome and unhappy, for in my heart I knew those lessons we had been preparing and which Dr. Hivale had been so anxious to print were not yet right—they would not prove to be the answer to India's need. It was the strangest, most painful, and before that sleepless night was over, the most blessed Christmas Eve of my life. For an invisible Friend crept up close to my aching heart and God and I passed the night talking to each other about the millions of India. We have all had the experience that the loneliest hours of life may prove to be the most precious. God sends us such lonely hours, so that he can fill the vacuum.

Christmas Day was as light-hearted as that night had been solemn. We enjoyed a wonderful celebration at Vadala, where Dr. Edward Fairbank and his family conduct one of the famous agricultural colleges of India. To have seen us in the midst of our fun on that day, nobody on earth would have guessed that all of us were missionaries and that none of us had imbibed anything stronger than tea. We were intoxicated with the spirit of Christmas.

THROUGH THE HEART OF HINDUSTAN AND THE PUNJAB

The next day a hundred delegates hurried together from all over India to attend the annual conference of the National Christian Council held at Nagpur. The chairman of the Council was the Bishop of Dornakal, and its secretary was President Roy Strock of Guntur. Out in front also sat the leader of the world Christian movement, Dr. John R. Mott. And there was Bishop J. W. Pickett, a foremost authority on the Christian mass movements of India. Indeed, I felt as if the gods on Olympus were holding a session. The discussion centered mainly around the depressed classes, who were clamoring to enter the Christian church and so to get out of their endless and hopeless depression.

Mr. Gandhi had written the Council a letter accusing missionaries of enticing the outcastes by picturing to them the worldly advantages they would gain by becoming

Christians. The Council spent the entire last day trying to word a reply so that it would not sound as if they were over-urging the outcastes but that still would make them feel welcome.

All this postponed my presentation of literacy to the last half hour. It seemed to me that the real issue was not whether we should or should not receive the outcastes into the church, but what kind of Christians we would make of them. We in America could not be very satisfactory Christians if we never read our Bibles nor other Christian literature. How can we expect these outcaste peoples, struggling against all their old habits, to be good Christians unless they can go to the Gospels daily to get victory by the power of Christ? Because of the mass conversions of the depressed classes the literacy of Christians in India had dropped six per cent in twenty years. This was something to worry about. If we receive them illiterate and leave them that way, we are cheating them, and we are risking the quality of the church and its standing in India.

To all this, the Council listened for the final twenty-five minutes, eyes on their watches, and then rushed off to catch their trains. They had at least done a little better by the then illiterate ninety-two per cent of India than any council that had ever gone before them.

Our next conference was at Baloda Bazar in the Central Provinces. Here two first-rate educators, the Reverends J. C. Koenig and E. W. Menzel, and some of their Indian teachers fairly scintillated with bursts of genius as they prepared a delightful key-word set of lessons. I know no other fun like making lessons with a really brilliant team.

Mr. Koenig had already prepared a list of the thousand most used Hindi words to guide writers of primers for children. These had been adopted by the Central Provinces government. Koenig's list revealed the words that books print oftenest but not the words that illiterates speak—it is amazing how these differ in India. After my visit, Mr. Menzel prepared another list of words by listening to illiterates talk and writing down the words they used. Hindi writers will henceforth have two excellent guides for preparing the kind of literature that adults just learning to read will love—if the fastidious Hindi scholars will tolerate in print words taken directly from the speech of the people. I doubt if they will, for the vernacular is full of slang! In America, being democratic, we soon adopt these words of lowly origin into the dictionary, but in India, never!

Koenig, Menzel, and I also tried another daring innovation—tampering with the Hindi alphabet; but we got into trouble. The reaction was like an erupting volcano. Hindi letters, the pundits let us know, have the most ancient and aristocratic lineage on earth, descending from sacred Sanskrit—a perfect alphabet handed down out of heaven. So we fled from holy ground like Adam from Eden, and never again ventured to tamper with alphabets. Somebody else can do that!

Mr. Jawaharlal Nehru, distinguished leader in the Indian National Congress, has since come out boldly in favor of using the Roman letters in all Indian languages. Under the protection of his shadow, I venture to endorse this with all my heart, mind, and strength.

At Shantiniketan, north of Calcutta, I had the rare privilege of meeting one of the world's greatest poets, the late Rabindranath Tagore, who was then very aged and looking like Father Time, with his long, white, flowing beard. When he looked at me with those large brilliant eyes, I forgot everything except the lovely soul behind them and the music of his sweet voice. He was the most unhurried great man I have ever met. For an hour I listened in rapt silence while he told me of his dream for Shantiniketan and the education of India.

One mark of Tagore's genius was this: that he took the common spoken words of Bengal's masses and wove them together into sentences of breath-taking beauty. He did it so long and so bewitchingly that the spoken Bengali has become correct as well as popular, and the old, stilted, "learned," cloudy language of the pundits has lost its grip on literature.

Tagore was the first in India to break the backbone of literary prudery. He set an example that writers in other dialects now venture to follow. Mr. Gandhi was doing it in his magazine *Harijan* for all India; we were indeed witnessing the beginning of a literary revolution that would prove to be a godsend to our literacy program. All over India I preached about Tagore, India's greatest living poet, as proof that all writers ought to become simple, clear, and direct, and Tagore's name convinced even the pundits.

At Allahabad, five hundred miles up the Ganges from Calcutta, Sam Higginbottom presides over his famous Agricultural Institute. One of the major concerns of Higginbottom and his colleagues from the first has been the improvement of India's cattle. India has the largest cattle population of any country in the world. No Hindu ever kills a cow. They have homes for aged, weak, and helpless cattle. But India's cows, unfortunately, give little milk, barely enough for their calves, and are used chiefly as draught animals for plows and carts. Higginbottom got the idea of introducing strains of great milk-producing cattle like Guernseys or Holsteins. The one hundred million cows that have been eating India into poverty would then become as much an asset as they have been a liability.

But Higginbottom's problem was that diseases in India killed foreign cows, whereas long exposure has rendered the Indian cattle almost immune to these diseases. So he had to find a way to cross native and foreign strains in such a way as to produce milk and at the same time retain immunity from disease.

It will require many generations of skillful breeding to establish these new cattle strains throughout India, but when it is accomplished it will have done more to furnish food for the starving multitudes than any other single step ever taken.

This huge undertaking requires the intelligent cooperation of the common people. It is impossible to go around and explain the principles to three hundred and forty-five million men and women by word of mouth, but it would be easy to enlist cooperation if only the people could read. This is why Sam Higginbottom said to his students at the end of my first lecture: "There has never been a more important subject discussed in this college than the one you have just heard."

Straight across the Jumna River from the Agricultural Institute is Ewing Christian College. Here were five hundred students burning with passion to lift India out of poverty and ignorance. They crowded the platform after I had challenged them to join the army of literacy teachers, and offered themselves, not one by one, but in platoons and companies. The statement that struck fire in their young souls was this:

"In five years there is going to be a tremendous awakening of interest in literacy throughout India, such as we now have in Russia, Turkey, Mexico, and China. Then India will be looking for leaders trained to become directors of adult education. Only a handful as yet meet the requirements. Thousands of writers will be needed also who know how to say things clearly and in simple, beautiful language such as Tagore uses in Bengali. Over a quarter of a million educated men and women in India are at present looking in vain for suitable employment. The number of available jobs for educated men and women is not as great as the supply. But this swiftly expanding literacy movement is a new field of opportunity for those who are adaptable and far-sighted enough to see what is ahead. You students will soon have a vacation; use it to gain the experience you will need by teaching illiterates in your community. Then you will be ready for the new day."

That appeal I found brought students to the platform in every part of India.

Dr. J. H. Lawrence of Mainpuri had had the longest experience in all northern India in teaching illiterates. He had a school for men, women, and children, from sixty down to six, and used his own key-word method similar to ours in Lanao. Dr. Lawrence was a genius as a story writer in the simplest Hindi dialect. He could write equally well for men, women, or children. Some of his tales were borrowed from foreign lands, but most of them were taken from Indian folklore. He had put the *Gospel of Luke* into Hindi without ever an unfamiliar word, and yet it was as faithful to the original as the difficult standard Hindi text.

"Indeed," he declared, "it is more faithful, for, as all Bible students know, the original New Testament was not written in the classical Greek. It was written in the spoken Greek of Christ's day—they called it *koinē*, but we call it 'lingo.' Unless we translate the New Testament so that it is equally simple in Hindi, we in turn are not being faithful to the lovely simplicity of the original. It is mistranslating clear writing into the unintelligible. We make people think the Bible is 'highfalutin' while in reality it was common folk's talk."

Lawrence was not only telling the truth, he was using good horse-sense.

At Agra I had the unforgettable experience of visiting

the Taj Mahal by moonlight. Gossamer clouds reached down out of the evening sky and hung over the tips of the Taj minarets as though one of the "many mansions" that Jesus spoke about had been let down out of heaven in a moonbeam net and might be lifted to heaven again.

Canon T. D. Sully, principal of St. John's College at Agra, went with me to see this loveliest of all human creations and entertained me in his home. The Canon looked like Hoffman's pictures of Jesus Christ, and his gentle voice and loving thoughtfulness were as Christlike as his appearance. His students had caught much of his compassion and were as pathetically eager to help India's illiterate unfortunates as the students in Allahabad had been. The day I was there they started a four-page paper in the simple language used by illiterate people and have carried it on ever since.

The Training School for Village Teachers at Moga, south of Lahore, deserves its reputation as the most modern educational institution in all India. Here I found the finest educational skill and something far deeper. Dr. and Mrs. Arthur E. Harper, graduates of Teachers College at Columbia University, and their highly trained Indian and American staff radiated a Christian spirit that even in a pugnacious province like the Punjab was bringing divergent elements into loving cooperation. For our conference at Moga, the Harpers had gathered Christians, Moslems, Hindus, and Jains, who worked in delightful companionship.

Here our aim was to make "each one teach one" lessons

in Urdu, which employs an Arabic form of alphabet. Half the vowels in Urdu are omitted, much as we use the abbreviation "bldg.," which one has to learn stands for "building" and not "bulldog." Urdu is almost as bad as English. In such a language there seemed to be no choice but to use the story method, beginning with easy sentences and building up a vocabulary by frequent repetition of familiar words. This is how Moga was teaching children. They had not up to that time attempted to teach adults. While I was there we tried to make lessons that could be taught to adults merely by following the line in the text, as a correspondence school makes self-explanatory lessons that the student can study by himself.

When we broke up five days later, I knew in my heart that we had not found the perfect answer to the riddle of Punjabi Urdu, but all of us parted smiling and happy, confident that we had started right and would finally succeed. We were happy, too, at the memory of the heavenly days we had enjoyed together.

Of all the precious memories at Moga, the one that went deepest into my heart was a conversation with Mr. Sadr-ud-din, Supervisor of Schools at Ferozpore. This Moslem gentleman was a rare spirit, overflowing with love and with a desire to do a million times more for India, for the whole world, than he knew how to do. He wanted me to realize how profoundly he was impressed by the life and teaching of Jesus Christ.

"The greatest story in the world," Sadr-ud-din told me with his eyes full of tears, "is the story of Jesus and the woman at the well. It has every quality of greatness. Jesus breaks the customs by talking to a woman alone, and transforms her life. Jesus meets this stranger of a hated race and a different religion, but he does not hesitate to break through every convention and talk to her, alone, and then he leaves her better than he found her. The greatest need of the whole world is to break down all the walls that separate us, of race and religion and nationality and sex, so that the pure love of God can tie the world together. The idea of God the invisible who is worshipped in spirit and in truth is the loftiest idea of God ever uttered. This story is so wonderful that I have it repeated to every child in every grade of my school. It strikes straight at the worst curse in India—the caste system."

The morning before I was to leave Moga, a truckload of students from the Government Training School in Lahore came down to visit this famous school. When I challenged these Lahore students to become specialists in literacy, they responded with eagerness, as only youth can. Several of them followed me back to Dr. Harper's home and insisted on knowing just how they could prepare for this new profession. One young man begged me to change my plans and go with him to Jind State, where his father was superintendent of schools. Two young men from Afghanistan demanded that I go to their country beyond the Khyber Pass at once. "We are far worse off than India," they said, "for we are one hundred per cent illiterate! We will make sure that our government sends you a special invitation." They stuck so close and pleaded so hard that I missed my lunch and had to carry it along to eat on the train. "God helping me," I told those boys, "I shall go to Afghanistan." And I mean to keep that promise.

In the ashram founded by Dr. E. Stanley Jones at Lucknow was another of those "heavens on earth" that have made my journeys so delightful. People of several nationalities and castes live together in radiant fellowship, some of them studying, others teaching, others laboring. All worship together. The prayer hours morning and evening, while we sat on the floor listening to God, filled my heart with a strange ecstasy, which comes back as I write. We could recover the sense of God's presence in America if we had a shrine in every Christian home and spent an hour in morning and evening prayer.

Mr. J. Holmes Smith, head of the ashram, was working actively in an organization to rescue the masses from debt and ignorance. Practically all the illiterate people in India are in debt, and since they cannot read they do not know what the account says; they only know that they and their ancestors have always been in debt and that they must do exactly what the money-lenders tell them. If that terrible load is lifted from the illiterate half of humanity, it will be one of the most glorious liberations in history.

At Isabella Thoburn College in Lucknow I asked the women students to make themselves specialists in lifting Indian women out of illiteracy. At somebody's suggestion we asked how many would volunteer to teach at least two and how many of them would try to write easy articles for illiterates to read. The whole roomful rose as though the floor had been lifted under them. After my talk they stampeded to the platform to volunteer, all of them asking questions at once. The terrible eagerness of India's educated young men and women holds the promise of the making of a new nation—one of the mightiest on earth; and India's wonderful young women will have an immense part to play.

The National Christian Council had by this time determined to take up literacy as one of its large programs, and in February, 1937, it called a national conference in Nagpur, the city where its headquarters are located. Many of India's leading educators were present. The findings of this conference were circulated over all India. Here there is space for only a few sentences from the stirring appeal with which the findings conclude:

Without the loyal service of patriotic young men and women, India cannot become literate. The insistent demand of the times is for youth who will gladly devote their time and effort to teaching illiterates in village and town as a great labor of love. We urge them to learn the best methods and carry the torch of education to their villages during the coming summer.

We pass on to them and to all our fellow-workers the ringing words of Garibaldi: "I offer neither pay nor quarters nor provisions; I offer hunger, thirst, forced marches, battles, and death. Let him who loves his country in his heart, and not with his lips only, follow me!"

I wrote in my diary on the final night of that conference: "Tired but thankful for the finish of a wonderful conference. Keep us humble and perfectly responsive, open wide toward thee. This I pray for myself and all the delegates who are again scattering over India. God, all thy will, for all of us!"

ANOTHER LANGUAGE AND A NEW METHOD

There was thrill after thrill in the visit the next week to the immense city of Bombay. Under Dr. John McKenzie's leadership a conference was held at Wilson College; then another under the auspices of the Educational Committee of the Bombay Representative Christian Council. At an official city mass meeting on literacy the chairman was Bombay's leading citizen, former Mayor K. F. Nariman. But the man who kindled our enthusiasm most was a Hindu visitor from the important city of Poona—its mayor, Mr. S. R. Bhagwat. God raised him up for this turning point in India's history. He is an engineer, but his leading passion is the salvation of the illiterate masses from their misery, and he is convinced that they must be taught to read and write so that they will be able to lift themselves. All over India I found such wonderful Hindus, aching to lift the load from their tragic country, men and women who have much to teach America in self-sacrificing devotion. Mr. Bhagwat was living in a modest little house and spending all his income for the masses.

These months had taught me that India needed a wholly different kind of lessons from those in our easy Moro language, but what the new thing was to be only God knew. I went to Godhra, north of Bombay, praying and nearly desperate. The faculty of the Teacher Training School there heartily cooperated and for two weeks concentrated on making lessons in Gujerati, the language of about twelve million people in the northern parts of Bombay Presidency and Baroda.

My diary reminds me how, like a drowning man, I was grasping at a straw. While I was praying at midnight an idea came to me and the next day we tried it. Fortunately at the Training School there was a good Indian artist and he did his best. We found words that began with each of the Gujerati consonants, then made pictures for the words and prepared the first "picture-word-syllable" chart of its kind in India—or the world.[1] Some women and children illiterates tried it and loved it so much they came back earlier every day for more. We would find them waiting on the doorstep when we arrived. God had answered prayer, for that week we turned a literacy corner not only for India but for many other nations.

At the urgent request of Mr. Ralla Ram, secretary of the Student Christian Movement of India, I postponed my sailing for Africa and hastened back to Allahabad for further experiments with our Hindi charts. He had collected several highly educated Indians, college professors with scientific training, men who were eager for new things, no matter how radical, if only they could save India.

My heart still warms at the memory of the magnificent spirit of that group, particularly Ralla Ram; I could feel him praying every minute we labored. Then there was

[1] See chart on opposite page.

GUJERATI READING CHART

Mr. Reyazul Hassan, a Moslem who worked all day in a government office. He would rush home from his office at five o'clock and work on with me in the evening until it was time to close the college buildings for the night. We rearranged the Urdu letters according to their shapes and then he made brilliant nonsense rhymes to assist our memories. After he got home at night Hassan tried these lessons on illiterates as long as they would stay awake, and returned every day thrilled at their success.

By the end of two weeks our committee had prepared one set of lessons in Hindi and another in Urdu unlike any we had ever done elsewhere. It is marvelous how working creatively on literacy lessons ties silver threads about our hearts. Time after time separating from my fellow-workers was harder than pulling out an eye tooth. The last session at Allahabad was a love feast and a prayer meeting of thanksgiving. When I left they gave me a silver acanthus leaf picture frame shaped like a heart and told me, "With this we are giving you India's heart."

Pundit Jawaharlal Nehru lived in Allahabad and had sent word that he was very anxious for us to work on lessons in Urdu, so I had the joy of taking the Urdu lessons to his home. He gave me the impression of great refinement and sensitiveness to the highest spiritual values. He afterwards wrote me as follows:

Anand Bhawan, Allahabad

I am greatly interested in the literacy movement which is gathering momentum in India. With your wide experience in the liquidation of illiteracy, this movement should derive great profit by your cooperation. I hope that the provincial governments in India, who are pushing this literacy campaign, will take full advantage of your expert knowledge and experience and will seek your cooperation. I am glad to learn that the World Literacy Committee of New York is interesting itself in the work in India. Any help that they may give in this work will be very welcome and will bear fruitful results.

> Yours sincerely,
> JAWAHARLAL NEHRU

With less than two weeks to spare before leaving for Africa, I hurried down to Sholapur and worked at the home of the Reverend William Hazen with feverish haste to throw into Marathi the new discoveries in "picture-word-syllable" chart-making that we had improved at Allahabad.[1] Every evening we went to a criminal tribe settlement to experiment and we found the new method gave better results than anything we had ever tried. Mrs. Hazen later wrote that "they work like a miracle."

With these lessons under my arm, I went back to Poona to show them to my friend, Mayor Bhagwat. Eager and impulsive as ever, he took me at once to his car and in fifteen minutes we were at the office of his printer! Mr. Bhagwat ordered ten thousand copies of the lessons made then and there, although I begged him to try out only a thousand first, for they most certainly needed improvement. "No, no," he said. "I can sell ten thousand as easily

[1] See chart on p. 128.

MARATHI READING CHART

बा	या	णा	ना
धा	झा	दा	धा
गा	जा	ळा	दा
खा	छा	ठा	था
का	चा	टा	ता

वाघ	या	खण	नाग
घर	झाड	ऊ	धाव
गाय	जोते	बस	दर
खार	छत्री	ताप	पाणी
बकरा	चाक	तळे	तार

as one thousand." So I surrendered. You can't put your foot down and say "no" to a mayor!

I had only two more days before leaving Bombay and was irresistibly driven by some power beyond me to undertake the preparation of lessons in the form of Urdu, commonly used among the Moslems of that city and surrounding region. Urdu is written in the Persian character and is the language generally spoken in Moslem centers of population. It has a number of variant forms in different parts of India. I sought some competent Moslem to help me and was fortunate in being introduced to a distinguished lawyer, Mr. A. H. Fyzee. His wife and mother, both educated women, caught my enthusiasm at once and worked with me all day Easter Sunday, except while I was in church. I felt that I had never pleased the Master more than that Holy Week, working all Good Friday with a Brahman and all Easter with two Moslem women. In two days' time we had completed our set of Bombay Urdu lessons.

Monday afternoon former Mayor Nariman and a large crowd of leading Indians met at the Gilder Tank School, the leading public school of Bombay, and listened to Mr. Bhagwat and myself describe the new lessons and tell them how Bombay might become literate. The government agreed to publish all of the new lessons in Marathi, Gujerati, Hindi, and Urdu. They began that afternoon to lay the foundation for what was two years later to be one of the most gigantic literacy campaigns in any city in all history.

As I sailed away from India that spring, bound for Africa, I wrote to my "prayer regiment," some hundreds of people scattered over all the world who have promised to pray for this literacy work every day: "Within five years a tremendous campaign against illiteracy will grip all India." And it did!

These are a few brief pictures of the second visit to India, but as I read over the diary that I was writing at the close of each day, I am reminded that the story you have read tells only of surface results, and that the deep secret of these remarkable days of discovery lies in surrender. On January 1, 1937, I had written in my diary:

God, I want to give you every minute of this year. I shall try to keep you in mind every minute of my waking hours. I shall try to let my hand write what you direct. I shall try to let you be the speaker to direct every word. I shall try to let you direct my acts. I shall try not to act nor speak nor even think except in cooperation with you.

A few days later I was writing again to my "prayer regiment":

These days have been closer to God than any five days of my life, and I want to make all 1937 like that, without a waking hour away from God. The thing that God has asked me to do for India and for the whole world will not be accomplished unless I make good on this new resolve. If God can only have his perfect chance, the thing he desires for India and for the illiterates of the world will come to pass.

CHAPTER SIX

A Fifty-Day Adventure in East Africa

LANDING at Mombasa, the principal port of Kenya, one takes an evening train for the long climb to Nairobi, the capital, a mile above sea level, and three hundred miles inland. The next morning one awakes to look out over a vast grassy plain where thousands of zebras, wildebeestes, gazelles, antelopes, and ostriches are grazing, unafraid of the train. One giraffe on the hillside towers against the sky—he looks tall enough to reach up and bite a piece out of the pale setting moon. On the south side of the track, extending for hundreds of miles, is a game preserve where nobody is allowed to hunt. The only enemies of these gentle-eyed grazing creatures are the lions, who, in defiance of the law, make a kill whenever they are hungry. Zebras are their delicacy, and they are never in want of fresh meat, for twenty-five millions of these beautiful black and white striped ponies range the African plains.

On that April afternoon in 1937 when I reached Nairobi, Mr. E. G. Norris, the Director of Education, promptly dispatched one letter to the Catholic bishop and another to a representative of the Protestant missions, requesting each of them to appoint two language experts to help build adult lessons.

Mr. Norris then sent me on to Kisumu, some two hundred miles west of Nairobi, with Archdeacon Owen, a leading missionary of the Church of England, a linguistic authority and a noted geologist. Once the archdeacon stopped his car to jump into a new excavation and study the stones. Presently he emerged in triumph, with a rough stone that he said was made by the most primitive people in the world.

"Are their descendants in Africa now?" I asked innocently, and he looked at me almost with pity.

"The lowest people on the earth today are highly civilized compared with those men of the rough stone age," he said. "They lived here a hundred thousand years ago. We may find that Africa was the cradle of the human race; this valley may have been the Garden of Eden." He chuckled at that.

In addition to his other gifts, the archdeacon had a fine sense of humor—a necessity for a missionary in Africa.

Kisumu is a town of shining white houses on the shore of Lake Victoria. My task was to make lessons in the Luo language, which belongs to the Sudan or Nilotic language group. There are three main language groups in Africa. The other two are Bantu and Hamitic. Archdeacon Owen introduced me to a great scholar of the Luo language, his friend Father Rolands of the Roman Catholic Society at

Kisumu, and the kindly father gave me a copy of his new Luo grammar—and his blessing.

The committee appointed to work with me was the faculty of the Maseno School for Boys, on the edge of the densely settled Kavirondo Reserve.

At night I slept on one side of the equator and during the day our committee worked on the other—a marker showed exactly where it crossed the school grounds. One evening, after looking in all directions to be sure nobody was watching, I stepped back and forth across the equator one thousand times—just so I could boast. It seemed that with the equator completely at one's mercy something had to be done about it. So, believe it or not, Mr. Ripley, I am the only living man—at least from Benton, Pennsylvania—who has crossed the equator one thousand times in twenty-five minutes.

At a wee place called Bunyori, in the bush north of Kisumu, the American Church of God has a mission among the Nyore people, who speak one of the Bantu languages. With a tiny hand-press and a small amount of type, an American woman and her faithful African helper had printed primers and booklets about geography and other subjects. They had translated the entire New Testament into Nyore, and it had been published by the American Bible Society. Their school is very practical, teaching the boys how to farm and build houses and the girls how to cook and weave and care for children.

Making lessons in Africa is much easier than in India, because the alphabets are so much simpler and more phonetic. There were almost no written languages south of the Sahara desert when the missionaries arrived; so they could choose their own alphabets. The only trouble is that there are many sounds in Africa for which we whites have no letters. You have doubtless read of the "kq" sound the Zulus use—a sound like saying "get up" to a horse by making a cracking sound behind your wisdom teeth. Spell that if you can! So if you had *three* cracking sounds to spell, as the Zulus have, what letters would you use? Perhaps "kq," "kqx," and "qxg"?

However, the big riddle in Africa is not how to spell, but what language to teach illiterates. "Their own language, of course," you say. Yes, but there are hundreds of languages and dialects that so shade into one another that it cannot be determined where one ends and the next begins. Some dialects are spoken by several million people, some by a few thousand. For example, in the section of Kenya where we were working, there are five different missionary societies from America and England, each working with a different dialect. All five dialects belong to the Bantu family and are enough alike for the native people to talk to one another with the aid of a few gestures. Did they need five different sets of lessons and five different newspapers? This was our problem. The saving in time and money would be enormous if we could use only one. The missionaries agreed to give their best scholars a year to compare their word lists and find out. By the end of the week we had made charts in Luo and in Nyore.

As I went a little farther south into the Kikuyu country

I began to touch the most important of all the Bantu languages in Kenya. Kikuyu is spoken by over a million people. My heart was stirred by the hardships suffered by their women. As soon as she can walk, a baby girl begins to carry all her little back can stand, holding the load with a strap running over her forehead. She learns to walk leaning far forward and her neck muscles become so strong that by the age of fifteen she may be able to carry two hundred pounds. This practice the government has tried to discourage by making sixty pounds the legal load for women as for men, but Kikuyu women refused to obey this, saying, "Who are we that we should be limited to the load a man is able to carry?" All over this land, one sees lines of these pack-carrying women leaning forward as they trudge along, up and down the steep hills. The Kikuyu never go around a hill. They prefer to go straight up and straight down to their destination.

Here among the Kikuyu we ran into another of those perplexing spelling questions. The Italian Fathers, who have a school and press at Nyeri, in North Kenya, have adopted the Latin spelling as used in Italy. The Protestants had sought the advice of German authorities and had adopted a very different spelling, especially for vowels. No one had ever succeeded in reconciling these two forms of spelling; so when I arrived, our committee had to choose between them.

The three educated Africans who constituted my committee for the Kikuyu language desired the Italian form of spelling, and I was quite satisfied, because there were only five vowels—the shorter the better, for quick learning. So we spelled our charts as words are spelled in Spanish and Latin.

These three Africans were on fire with eagerness for the education of their people. I want their names in this book: Mr. Eliud W. Mathu, president, and Mr. James S. Gechuru, secretary, of the Kikuyu African Teachers' Union, both teachers in the Alliance High School; and Mr. Stevenson Githi, an educated evangelist of the Scottish Church Missions on an adjacent hill.

Building lessons with these young men was a spiritual benediction, for they were intensely in earnest. We were four brothers together, getting an immense thrill out of our adventure. They brought some near-by illiterates every day, and the lessons proved easier than anybody had expected. The teachers and students laughed in sheer glee. When we reported our good results to the Director of Education, he said: "You do not surprise me, for to tell you the truth, the African children are doing better in our schools than the white children."

He called a literacy conference at the Jeanes School in Kabete, and thirty-six persons responded, most of them Protestant and Roman Catholic missionaries. The three men who had helped build the Kikuyu lessons told the gathering that every African longs to become literate, and begged us to cooperate. "All we Africans ask of you whites is to give us your backing and financial help, and we will do the rest."

When the Chief Inspector took me to lunch later, he

said, "You little realize how timely your visit to Kenya has been. These Africans are getting more and more insistent that the government educate adults. We cannot refuse much longer."

The memory of those three African teachers pleading with us to help their illiterate countrymen came back to me some days afterward as I chatted with a handsomely dressed European while waiting in a railway station. He told me he was an official of a gold mining company, and when I told him my mission, he said, "I have nothing whatever against you personally, but I will tell you frankly that professionally you are my enemy. If you teach these savages to read, they will soon think they are as good as we are. Can't you see that you will start unrest and labor troubles all over Africa?"

This man who called himself my "enemy" had helped me for the first time to realize all it could mean to be one more missionary laboring for the emancipation of Africa. That night I wrote in my diary:

April 30, 1937: Today, Father, closes the four most glorious months of my life. We are stepping into a new world, dear Lord, hand in hand, sailing together with thrilling eagerness toward unknown shores. At fifty-two, nothing I have ever done seems worth preserving or even recalling save this high adventure. God, help me to continue a gentle but incessant pressure of my will toward thee on and on and on!

My hosts at the Alliance High School, Kikuyu, had been Principal Bruce Grieves and his wife, who had welcomed me like a long-lost son. When I was ready to leave they drove me all the way down to Nairobi, and waved to me as the train departed until we were out of sight. We had found each other on levels far deeper than common educational interests.

A short passage southward along the coast brought me to Zanzibar. This is the island to which, for centuries, most of the slaves taken in eastern Africa by Arab slave traders were brought to be auctioned off and shipped to various parts of the world. The Episcopal cathedral now stands on the site of the old slave market. Swahili is a Bantu language that contains many Arabic words. It was spoken on the coast and spread into the interior with the traders.

In 1890, when the British made Zanzibar a protectorate, they abolished slavery; but Swahili, the old slave drivers' language, has stuck. It has penetrated deep into the very heart of Africa and to this day it is the language people find it easiest to use when they visit tribes other than their own. The British are promoting Swahili as a *lingua franca* for East Africa. It has a comparatively simple grammar with few irregularities, and so is easy for Africans to learn—far easier for them than English. Yet the Africans outside Zanzibar prefer English, even if it is harder to learn, because one cannot secure advancement into the better paid government posts without command of it.

I discovered that the Director of Education, Mr. G. B. Johnson, and his wife had traveled in the United States studying educational methods and knew something of American education, and that Mrs. Johnson had founded and is principal of the government school for Moslem girls, one of the best of its kind to be found anywhere. They immediately drew together a fine, live committee, which in three days prepared eight Swahili lessons, tested them, and found that they worked with natives.

But our work was interrupted during the week of the coronation of King George VI. In Zanzibar I was staying in the home of the British Resident, the senior British official. He took me with him to the cathedral for the coronation service, and, to my horror, conducted me up to the front row, the only man in this group not wearing a military or academic costume. "At least," I thought, "I can stand for democracy!" The rest of that day was spent with the Resident and his wife, listening over the radio to the coronation ceremonies in London.

In the evening we went out to the enormous military grounds where thirty-six different African tribes, each forming its own circle, were dancing, singing, and shouting to celebrate the crowning of the new king. This, shades of Mr. Barnum, *was* "The Greatest Show on Earth," a thirty-six ring circus, every ring different from every other, out of the heart of Africa; drums, shields, spears, gorgeous head-dresses, hideous false faces, blood-curdling yells, war dances, love dances, spirit dances.

The coronation exercises interfered with our literacy efforts for nearly a week. Everybody celebrated; nobody felt in the mood to work. The only thing our energetic director, Mr. Johnson, could accomplish was to appoint committees.

As chairman of a special committee for work with women, Mrs. Johnson took me one day to the balcony of her school for a glimpse of the two hundred girls, rich and poor alike, some wearing fine dresses and jewelry, who come to school in tightly curtained motor cars.

"Now," she said, "I want you to prepare short-cut lessons with Arabic letters for these girls to use." So the next day a Moslem committee joined me and built up Swahili lessons with Arabic letters. The committee disagreed and scolded and shouted and ended up happy and triumphant, in true Arabian style.

The next stop on my voyage down the coast was Dar es Salaam, capital of the British mandated territory of Tanganyika. In the government school for African boys, three students helped build Swahili lessons several steps beyond any we had previously attempted. We gave them the name "Picture-Word-Syllable" lessons.[1] There were many more pictures than we had ever before used; indeed, one for every syllable in the Swahili language. The African boy who drew the pictures was only a fair artist, but his heart was in his task. He labored for many hours, patiently changing every picture as we changed our ideas. He felt that he was doing something enormously important for his needy people and insisted that he must give nothing but his best. Long before we had finished, this African boy had stolen my affections.

When we tried the Swahili lessons on illiterates, the

[1] See *Toward a Literate World*, by Frank C. Laubach, pp. 128-131. New York, World Literacy Committee, 1938.

pictures did so much of the teaching that after a few minutes of explanation the students could go on alone, discovering the sounds of the letters for themselves—and having great fun doing it.

My diary gives a better picture of the exciting days that followed at Dar es Salaam than I know how to show in any other way:

May 21, 1937: Yesterday and today have filled my heart with boundless gratitude to God. The new charts are working like magic! We have tried them on twelve or more persons with uniformly striking success. They are, I am sure, an improvement on anything we have ever before attempted. They contain sixty pictures and will involve a little more expense for cuts than I had hoped would be necessary, but they work!

I have a good place in which I can experiment with a large number of women. It is the African Girls' School, where a class for adult women is held every afternoon from two to four. These women seem to be even more eager to learn to read than the men are, and their progress has been astonishing.

They are not like the carriers of burdens that I saw in the Kikuyu hills. They are well clothed. But mentally and morally and spiritually they are pitiful. They are among the forty thousand natives who have been attracted from tribal life somewhere deep in Africa to live in this crowded city of Dar es Salaam. The men work, but their wives are cooped up in hot little rooms with nothing to do. Under these circumstances, they are under great temptation to break away from moral restraint, yet not one of them seems beyond hope if the vision of Christ can take possession of her life.

May 23: How eager they are to learn! Saturday afternoon came and the school was not to be open. The women begged me to return and arranged especially for the room. They don't want a holiday! I am weary after a two-hour session every afternoon, but they say, "We are not tired yet," and want to go on studying until dark.

The three leading African men of Dar es Salaam came to see this women's class this afternoon and showed great enthusiasm. These men are employed by the government but will give me their entire holiday, Monday. I am now teaching men in the forenoon in "The Old Comrades' Club House" and devoting the afternoon to this women's school. I have not seen such eagerness on the part of illiterates since I left Lanao!

May 27: Our Swahili lessons are all finished. Everybody, including two men over fifty years old, learned without the slightest difficulty. Eight men have reached the reading stage this week. One young fellow was learning the syllables when suddenly he discovered that he could pronounce new words alone. With victory gleaming in his eyes, he shouted: "Give me a book! I can read!" And he did, as elated as Columbus was when he first sighted the coast of the New World.

This forenoon Mr. Isherwood, Director of Education, called together sixty leaders, over half of them Africans, to "The Old Comrades' Club House" to hear the eight men who had studied there that week read and to lay plans for the future. I prayed and thanked God while those men demonstrated their brilliance before the meeting. "These men knew how to read before. They deceived you," insisted some of the English visitors, "for it is humanly impossible for anybody to read so soon." The faces of the new literates were radiant. When I said, "You may go now," they insisted on staying; and although they could not understand a word of English, they leaned forward and tried to learn it that afternoon. They had made up their minds that education was easy! "Look at the light in their eyes," whispered the Director of Education, and the light was in his eyes, too.

After that demonstration everybody was in favor of going ahead at once. The Africans, trembling with hope, said they would teach everybody in Dar es Salaam. We asked the men who had just learned to read if they would be teachers, too, and they nodded their heads and beamed like angels in heaven. Mr. Martin Kyamba, the outstanding African of all Tanganyika, clung to my hand and said in front of that whole gathering of foreigners, "I have watched you day by day teaching my countrymen, and I am convinced that this is the greatest hope that has come to Africa since Livingstone!"

We must have a newspaper for those newly literate men and women; we are agreed about that. The Director told us that he had had an interview with the governor, who had expressed himself as in favor of the paper, under proper auspices.

June 1 (sailing from Africa for India): Mr. John, editor of the government school paper, *Mamba Leo,* came with me as far as Zanzibar to make plans. Within half an hour after our arrival there, I was captured by the Moslem committee, who were full of new ideas for making better lessons with Arabic script. We had time to examine a new arrangement of letters, and they promised that they would finish the lessons themselves. The intense and passionate zeal of these Moslems for their faith and their people is beyond praise.

Mr. Johnson called his Zanzibar committee, and Mr. John told them that the Tanganyika government was ready to go full speed ahead. Then the committee decided to have a hundred copies of our lessons duplicated so that teachers in Kenya, Zanzibar, and Tanganyika might experiment and present their opinions to the directors, who will then decide whether to release appropriations to print the lessons on a large scale. Only a hundred copies on a duplicator! But no African leader was there to weep!

Now I am steaming away from Africa with no doubt about our lessons but much doubt about our organization and the training of our leaders. To the last hour before the boat sailed, four of the men who are to do the real work remained with me on the ship's deck to learn all they could. A cold chill is gripping my heart lest red tape strangle our new-born campaign to death.

«««»»»

I almost got back to Africa in 1940, but not quite. The World's Sunday School Association had invited me to speak and train literacy leaders at its proposed convention in Durban, South Africa, and I had planned to visit all southern and central Africa during the six months following the convention. But meanwhile the war between

Britain and Germany broke out and the Durban convention was canceled.

This first visit to Africa, like my first visit to India, was little more than exploratory and altogether too brief. The infant campaign did not thrive alone. In Kenya it was nearly choked to death by a controversy over spelling. The Protestants stood firm for the spelling that they had adopted in 1931, while the Kikuyu African Teachers' Union favored the spelling of the Italian Catholic Fathers. "The government," says the Union in a report, "was ready to print the lessons on a large scale . . . but unfortunately was unable to proceed on account of the orthography controversy." Behold what a great fire two letters can kindle! The Italian Fathers printed and used the new lessons without waiting for the government.

In spite of the disappointments, delays, and general indifference that have checked the efforts for extending adult literacy in Africa, some amazing reports have been received in the years intervening since that visit. At least forty mission stations have informed us that they have built lessons generally similar to those developed in 1937 and that they are being used with excellent results. There are doubtless others of which we have no record. Experience in the war has made many Africans aware of the importance of reading. A missionary serving as a chaplain with native troops somewhere in East Africa wrote in 1942 to Miss Margaret Wrong of the International Committee on Christian Literature for Africa: "You would be amazed at the sale of literature among African soldiers. It beats anything I have ever seen in the villages. I simply cannot keep pace with the demand. When work is over, a walk round the camps would show groups of Africans here and there reading, singing, and some studying, the place littered with books. It is the finest extra-mural university I have yet seen in Africa."

The experience in lesson building at Dar es Salaam marked a real advance in our world literacy program because it registered a definite improvement in method, the principal features of which might be thus summarized:

In India our pictures had illustrated all of the consonants, but only one of the vowels. Each consonant was followed by the vowel sound "a"; pictures illustrated the syllables "ba," "ma," "sa," and the rest, but not "be," nor "bi," nor "bo," nor "bu."

In the Swahili charts made in Dar es Salaam we had pictures of words that began with every possible combination: "ba," "be," "bi," "bo," "bu," "ma," "me," "mi," "mo," "mu," and so on to the end. While the Swahili charts required more pictures than the Indian charts used, they gave the student a picture for every syllable, so that if he forgot the sound, he could find it for himself. Our lessons in India had been like speeding down a fine asphalt road fifty miles an hour and suddenly running into mud holes. In Africa we had filled the holes. I left Zanzibar for Bombay determined that for our campaigns in India we would perfect lessons as smooth as those we had developed in Dar es Salaam.

SIXTEEN DAYS IN SOUTH INDIA

I arrived in Bombay on June 12, 1937, with plans to meet Mrs. Laubach in Colombo sixteen days later and proceed with her to Manila. I was so consumed with eagerness to accomplish many tasks in these brief weeks that I could not sleep. First I hurried down to Sholapur and told my good friends the Hazens of my hopes for the coming days. In two hours I was at work with a teacher and an artist, who shared some of my excitement, though they did not know what it was all about. In two days we changed our earlier Marathi lessons to conform to the African type of charts. Without taking time to try them on illiterates I started east to Hyderabad, in my pocket a letter of introduction to the Director of Education, intending to attempt the preparation of lessons in Urdu.

The Director was not there—providentially! From that point on I had the most astonishing experience of God's doing everything while I looked on that ever came to me. Walking toward the station I whispered, "Why did you bring me here, Lord? The Director isn't here." An inner voice said, "Go into this store." I looked and saw it was the British and Foreign Bible Society. I told the clerk my name and he cried, "We all know you. Come with me to Dr. Frank Sackett's home. He is the Methodist superintendent."

The moment my name was mentioned, Dr. Sackett picked up *Letters by a Modern Mystic* from his table and said, "I was just reading this. Will you go with me to Medak, seventy-five miles north of here?"

"I have just three days," I said.

"Then," he replied, "we will start immediately."

Medak is in the center of one of the greatest mass movements toward Christianity and is the seat of a normal training school. The faculty had not dreamed of my coming, but they stopped school at noon and set free eighteen missionaries and Indian teachers to make literacy lessons in Telugu. They made Miss Sallie Anstey, head of the Girls' Training School, "general" of this literacy army, and she was a wonderful general of a wonderful army. She prayed every minute and worked while she prayed.

The "war" began right after lunch and was carried on with unflagging spirit until eleven that night. Though the whole plan for Telugu was new and difficult, we all seemed able to take every step without a moment's hesitation. If God ever in this world inspired human beings, he gave us those lessons. Eight of us prepared the material, ten copied the letters by hand (for nobody has yet invented a typewriter that will hold all the Telugu letters), and two Indians drew pictures. Next day we worked all day until eleven at night, and on the third day we finished.

The air was electric; everybody felt sure that God was doing the work, using our hands and minds. The memory of those three days still makes me tingle. Later, when my co-workers tried the lessons on illiterates, they called them "miraculous," "perfect."

In that group was Frank Whittaker, who became secretary of the National Christian Council of India a few months later and who was responsible for setting up the splendid schedule for the literacy campaign of the following year. Its tremendous success is due more to his unquenchable zeal and infinite pains than to any other factors, and his zeal was born in Medak during those three days.

What God says to me through that miraculous experience is this: "You don't have to be bright; you don't have to be powerful; you don't have to see the whole way ahead. All you need is to be sure of what I want done, trust enough to venture, and obey every minute."

I now rushed on down to Bangalore in Mysore State to undertake the preparation of charts in Kanarese, an important language spoken by eleven million people, in which I had never before attempted lessons. I arrived unannounced, but the Methodist missionaries dropped everything else, found a drawing master, and set to work with me.

The Indian Director of Education, Mr. N. S. Subla Rao, returned the next day from his vacation and immediately became excited when he saw the lessons we had made. It happened that one of the most brilliant educators in India, K. Srinivasa Achar, Hindu headmaster of the Government Normal School in Tumkur, Mysore, was visiting the office when I came in. The Director appointed him on the spot to help me. He canceled his plans to return to his normal school and worked with us two more days. The Kanarese lessons were as fine as the Telugu, and the artist's work was better. That evening I left for Madras, my soul blazing with eagerness to throw just one more language, Tamil, into the new African type of lessons before leaving India.

The Christian Literature Society of Madras appointed their two best Tamil writers and critics and their expert artist to cooperate with me, and in two and a half days we had finished the Tamil lessons. That night I took the train for Colombo and could sleep! Between June 12 and 28 we had completed lessons in four languages along the new lines developed first in Dar es Salaam, and I knew it could be done all over India!

This is from a letter to my "prayer regiment," written after the ship left Colombo:

I am most grateful to God and to the people everywhere who dropped their work and closed their classes in order to help make lessons. Everywhere people seem to have heard about literacy and to be on tiptoe with expectancy for the future. I can hardly wait two years to hear, or—as I ardently hope—to see what the results will be.

It must seem to you like sheer audacity for me to have undertaken to help other countries with only my Philippine experience. But, after all, God, who had planned it all, pushed me on when I hardly knew what I was doing —and he is working out the future far ahead of us. We have nothing to fear except our own deafness to his voice when he calls us to larger opportunities. This much I can see—our experiments will have a profound significance for three-fifths of the human race. We are now en route to the Philippines to resume our work among the Moros— we can hardly wait. . . .

CHAPTER SEVEN

The India-wide Campaign for Literacy

U PON returning to Lanao we developed a new series of lessons based on what we called the "picture-chain" method,[1] even simpler than those we had developed in Africa. I was eager to try these all over India. The opportunity came in December, 1938, when the International Missionary Council met at Tambaram, near Madras.

Those two previous visits had sown more seed than any of us could have anticipated, and this third visit found the harvest ripe. The newspapers all over India had been giving our aims and efforts large publicity. Thousands of leaders who had formerly despaired of making that vast country literate were now convinced that the way had been found, and at the top of the list were Mr. Gandhi and Mr. Nehru. The imagination of the country was captured by figures showing the speed with which India could achieve literacy, if only enough public spirit and altruism could be released so that each literate would teach one

[1] See chart on p. 152.

amo	a	i	o	u
mama	ma	mi	mo	mu
sapi	sa	si	so	su
karabao	ka	ki	ko	ku
tali	ta	ti	to	tu
babak	ba	bi	bo	bu
lapad	la	li	lo	lu
nanas	na	ni	no	nu
papanok	pa	pi	po	pu
gantang	ga	gi	go	gu
dado	da	di	do	du
rantai	ra	ri	ro	ru
ngari	nga	ngi	ngo	ngu

MARANAW PICTURE-CHAIN CHART

Developed in 1938

illiterate a year—or, failing that, if he would pay somebody to do it for him:

In 1938—8% were literate. If each of the 8% taught one that year, then

      In 1939— 16% would be literate, and
      In 1940— 32% would be literate, and
      In 1941— 64% would be literate, and
      In 1942—128% would be literate!

That extra 28% would make up for the increase in population!

Of course this is pure idealism. We had not expected them to reach that perfect result, but they did better than ever before in their history. It is estimated on the basis of the 1941 census figures that the percentage of literates for the entire country increased from less than 7 per cent in 1931 to 12 per cent in 1941.

Frank Whittaker had arranged two hundred and eighteen meetings of various kinds preceding and following the Madras conference, and these proved to be the most wonderful experiences I had in India. Merely to name them, a line to a meeting, would take many pages of this book, and to do them justice would take a larger book than this.[1] I shall ask you to take grasshopper leaps with me to a score of the most interesting points, which must serve as samples for all the rest.

[1] *India Shall Be Literate*, sponsored by the National Christian Council of India, Nagpur, 1940, contains a history of the literacy movement in India and an account of the results of the meetings that followed Madras.

The early part of December, 1938, found me packed in a small auto with my friend Mason Olcott and his wife and children, going west through the hills of Madras Presidency until at last we came to a huge valley across which the government had just completed a mile-long dam for one of its wonderful irrigation projects (Britain was building such dams in India before we began them in America). Mason Olcott had selected Mettur Dam as the site for a literacy conference because it was accessible from eastern and western cities and because every delegate would be so far from home that he would not be bothered by his neighbors!

One hundred leading Hindus, Moslems, and Christians had come great distances, some over two hundred miles, to this remote place to plan the conquest of illiteracy. Religious differences were wholly forgotten while these men struggled with "public enemy number one"—as the Vice-Chancellor of the University of Madras called it in his opening speech. He had come one hundred and fifty miles to preside.

We did not try to make lessons—with a hundred leaders, all eager to talk, we would never have finished. We were there to wrestle with the other problems to be solved in carrying a literacy campaign through to victory— questions that will interest and perhaps astonish you.

There was a debate on the question whether "each one will really teach one." This gave us a chance to say that this will work if we can inject enough Christlike love into the campaign—and Hindus and Moslems believed it!

We discussed the high art of making adults love their teacher and their lessons so much they would come back without compulsion.

Somebody objected that adults were too old to learn, whereupon Mason Olcott brought forth Professor Edward L. Thorndike's *Adult Learning* to prove that a man of forty can learn more quickly than a child of six. A whole half day was devoted to women—only four per cent of the women of India are literate as against twelve per cent of the men.

A forenoon was dedicated to explaining how to start campaigns, how to get the people stirred up and eager, how to find teachers and generals, how to find the best time of day and the best places to teach, and how to get factories and schools and churches into the campaign.

But half the battle for literacy depends upon the literature that is prepared for the new literates. It must be *easy*. So the conference appointed language experts to prepare lists of the basic words the illiterates have been accustomed to using. It must be *interesting*, for semi-literates cannot read fast nor far—they want no scholarship, but simple, clear, high-powered news—every sentence packed with important facts. So we spent some hours in a fascinating and hilarious exploration of what illiterates talk about most. The list those men made astonishes and sometimes shocks Americans: debt and hate of money-lenders, Gandhi, jewelry for ladies' noses and ankles, fate, cows, cooking, cow dung for fuel, quarrels (especially of mothers and daughters), court trials, rice, pilgrimages and sacred rivers, ghosts, caste, everything about sex including birth control, riddles, sleight-of-hand and snake charming, eye diseases, itch, plague, purdah, weddings, water, selling girls, markets, snake bites, gossip, drowning, taxes, mud houses, rats.

We also discussed the question Mr. Gandhi had raised: Shall we fill people's stomachs and give them better homes first, or teach them to read first? The conference ended up unanimous on that question—if we make people literate, they will be able to help themselves, but if twelve per cent of India tries to lift the other eighty-eight per cent, it will never get done. As a grand climax the committee on findings read such a challenge to India as sent us home bursting with confidence and eagerness to get at the job. Mason Olcott's face was beaming. He had spent endless hours and much money in the interests of literacy and now his day of triumph had come.

Conferences like this in Mettur Dam were held in forty other parts of India during the succeeding five months, each lasting from a day to a week. Always there was a premier or vice-chancellor or mayor or judge or some other distinguished citizen in the chair. Always we discussed alphabets, looked wistfully at the Roman letters— but only twice dared to adopt them! Always teachers sat open-mouthed at the "revolutionary" idea that you can teach by love instead of by scolding. Always we had to prove the equally revolutionary idea that adults are not too old to learn. Always we had to answer the doubt as to whether people can be made unselfish enough to teach anybody else without pay. Often we had to face the doubt as to whether women ought to be allowed to read or had the brains to learn. Always the pundits insisted on using only those words to be found in classical literature—and always they were silenced by the example of Rabindranath Tagore and Gandhi. Between conferences were sessions for building lessons, making addresses of all kinds, holding interviews, and paying respects to officials.

This journey was broken between December 12 and 29 by the meeting of the International Missionary Council at Tambaram, a suburb of Madras. Four hundred and sixty-four delegates from sixty-nine nations and areas here wrestled with the overwhelming religious and social problems of our age. It was the first international conference of evangelical Christians in which a full half of the delegates were from the non-white peoples of the world and represented the younger churches. Furthermore, it was the first great Christian convention that gave any attention to the illiterate three-fifths of the world as a class.

The Literature Committee included these paragraphs in its findings:

Thus far we have discussed the needs of those who can read. But over ninety per cent of the adherents of non-Christian religions are illiterate. What is equally distressing is that in some lands many Christians, including some of their leaders, are unable to read their own Bibles and hymn books. It is futile to talk of distributing literature to these people until they can read.

As medicine heals the bodies of men, literacy liberates their minds and has a legitimate place in the Christian program.

To be successful, literacy campaigns must follow well tested scientific methods, and should have the best available expert advice on such matters as lesson building, basic word lists, adult psychology and the training of leaders. Invaluable experience has accumulated from the lands now engaged in the intensive literacy campaigns and provision must be made for passing on the experience to all regions grappling with the problem of illiteracy.

Those who have just learned to read must be supplied with a literature simple in form and interesting to adults. The need for this is acute, for if Christian writers fail to provide it many anti-Christian forces will enter the field. Such a literature calls for expert authorship, and help in this matter should be afforded from one field to another.

The meeting was crowded with notable speeches that stirred one's very depths. The climax was Dr. John R. Mott's marvelous closing address, which sent us out silent with aching purpose.

Between sessions delegates came to the literature room where fifty literacy lessons were exhibited and where the beginnings were made of twelve more picture-chain charts in languages of Africa, Asia, and the Americas. At the same time a fine artist from the Christian Literature Society of Madras prepared on a type of plastic board called Masonite a large picture-chain chart in the Tamil language. It was beautifully painted in three colors and shimmered with a special kind of varnish, the loveliest chart any of us had ever seen. This I carried with me all over India and it sold the picture-chain method by its sheer beauty.

The first place we showed this chart following the Madras conference was at Bangalore, Mysore State. Dr. Fred Field Goodsell, executive vice-president of the American Board of Commissioners for Foreign Missions, went with me to show it to the Dewan (Premier), Sir Mirza M. Ismael, B.A., K.C.I.E., O.B.E. The Dewan is an engineer whose remarkable development of Mysore State makes one feel he deserves all those honors. He is a lover of beauty and was charmed by our beautiful chart. "Make one of these for us in Kanarese," he said, "and we will have it made up on green Mysore marble with inlaid letters in silver and placed in every village in our dominion!"

The Dewan requested me to go to Mysore City, of which he is tremendously proud. These Indian States are totalitarian, and the request of a dewan is a command! I obeyed, and was entertained like a prince at the government palace. In the evening I was taken to see the most marvelous system of illuminated, colored fountains in all India, or, so far as I know, in all the world—the Dewan's cherished creation. The fountains are located below the great dam that furnishes lights to all Mysore cities and will soon, the Dewan said, be lighting every village home in the state. The sheer ability of these government officials in Mysore, and the clip, clip with which they were running everything was marvelous. There was here no sign of democracy, but a most competent and benevolent dictatorship, if one may judge by material progress.

Early in January, 1939, I returned to Madras to meet fifty-five of the élite gathered at the beautiful home of Mrs. Ammu Swamanathan. The Premier of the Madras provincial government, C. Rajagopalachari, was chairman. Later he came into wider fame for his independent utterances in the Indian Congress. The president of every leading college in Madras was present. This literacy adventure, which two years before had been confined almost wholly to missionaries and Christian laymen, was now drawing hearty support from leaders of all the Indian communities. Wholly overwhelmed at the hospitality of Madras society, I wrote in my diary that evening:

O God, O God, these twenty millions of illiterate Tamils hang now upon that group who have met here with the Premier to organize the Adult Education Movement of Madras Presidency. Thou knowest how to prepare their hearts to do what thou dost desire. Please, God, take such possession of me that thy will, exactly, all and nothing but thy perfect will, may be accomplished. This is thy work and it must go on. Others are now seeing the vision and they will continue it. Thank thee, dear Friend, for letting me have a share in this stupendous undertaking.

In the magnificent buildings of Madras University was held the South India Adult Education Conference. The presiding officer was the Minister of Education. Educators of every religion spoke, but above them all the Christian leaders—Mrs. A. Devasahayam, Mr. S. G. Daniel, and Dr. Mason Olcott—shone like stars. These three, one felt, represented the passion of Christ spending itself for the oppressed. But the undying fire in their hearts was matched by a young Hindu, Mr. T. J. R. Gopal, a passionately patriotic youth who had organized this conference and who later wrote a book about it. Heaven had set his young heart literally on fire with passion to get the Tamil people literate, and with the impatience of youth he wanted no time lost in doing it!

As we journeyed north again we stopped at Raichur in Hyderabad State, where a hundred Christians and a dozen missionaries were gathered to do further work on our Kanarese lessons, and to learn to teach them. I told them the Dewan of Mysore said he would make our charts on marble if we prepared good ones. Two students were artists. A dozen others were chosen to work. It was one of the most exciting weeks of this breath-taking year. No, not a week—only three days! We all worked until midnight every night and until three in the morning the last day, to get the pictures done in colors before my departure. Everybody was so happy with the results that we nearly wept on each other's shoulders. Before I left they put a lovely blue Kashmir shawl around my shoulders and said, "With this shawl we adopt you. Now you are an Indian!" I carry that shawl with me everywhere and wrap it around me when I pray for India. They sent Mrs. Laubach a lovely red one to match it.

The Director of Education of the little state of Aundh, near Hyderabad, telegraphed that their *rajkumar* (prince) wanted me to come. There was not a day available, so I had to say "no." But Aundh State, prince and all, had caught the literacy epidemic and went ahead so effectively that they outdistanced any other state in India so far as percentages were concerned. The school children were all dismissed for three months to help teach the illiterates. Their slogan was: "Everybody in the state literate in twelve weeks!" The *rajkumar* took a leading part in the campaign, going with his princess from village to village, singing *kirtans* (long musical narratives) on literacy. There were large phonetic charts posted in conspicuous places in every village. All the villagers gathered round these centers at night to study. In two months twelve thousand learned to read out of a total population of seventy-six thousand. Literacy had been doubled in eight weeks. If a little state can do that, why not a big one?

At Jubbulpore, in the Central Provinces, I found a hundred literacy students gathered on the veranda of Leonard Theological Seminary, teaching one another. As soon as they learned a lesson they had to teach it to the newest students. This school had begun with about ten pupils who had brought others each evening until it spilled all over the Seminary yard.

The students of eight other schools in that city responded to a challenge to overthrow India's illiteracy by volunteering almost to the last man. A professor of Robertson College took me and twenty students with him to a village a few miles from Jubbulpore where his class is helping in social reconstruction. The students learned how to use the new charts for teaching illiterates, while all the village folk were eager and excited with the prospects of learning to read. Thereafter literacy was central in their village uplift project, as it is in fifty other college projects in India.

In the hill country of Chota Nagpur, at Ranchi, we made picture-chain lessons in the Mundari language and showed them to five hundred representatives from Lutheran, Anglican, and Roman Catholic churches, and the government schools. All came together in the Anglican church—Catholics as well as Protestants. It seemed as if the millennium were at hand. The very fact that Christians who had never spoken to one another before had found a common task to perform for India gave them a new sense of oneness.

In St. John's Hall, which is a Roman Catholic school at Sindega, near Ranchi, I demonstrated the Mundari lessons to three hundred people. They said they already had fifteen thousand illiterates under instruction. The Catholic fathers were eager and excited about the possibilities of literacy.

Patna, capital of Bihar Province, which I visited in February, was the buzzing scene of one of the world's greatest literacy campaigns. Mr. B. B. Mukherjee had started it and was its secretary. He told me how he had "caught the literacy bug." His wife had attended a Girl Guides' convention at Calcutta, where she had heard about the Philippine method of teaching and about the rapid progress of the Moros. On fire with enthusiasm, she returned home and aroused her husband's interest in the cause of literacy. That is one of the amazing aspects of India, that so many men and women become aflame with an unquenchable passion to make their people literate and to lift them out of poverty.

The city of Patna was alive with literacy campaigns. Mr. Mukherjee took me from one to another until I was nearly dead and then said we had barely started! I saw classes in Hindustani and Urdu being taught side by side. These two languages are really the same language in Bihar, only the alphabets are different, for Moslems will have nothing but Persian letters and Hindus will have nothing but those derived from Sanskrit. All they had to do was to use the same lesson text in different alphabets! I saw some of the students learning both alphabets at once and having fun doing it. Everywhere in Bihar the literacy classrooms were packed to suffocation with students. As I looked into their pathetic faces, I could think only of the helpless, defeated look of cattle in a slaughter house. India does not know how to smile, for she has had so little to smile about.

With Mr. Mukherjee I attended a huge gathering where the volunteer teachers were wedged in against each other, as everybody tried to see the instruction of illiterates. The climax at Patna was a meeting in a gigantic hall where I had to shout to be heard by the crowd of a thousand people who were present, the élite of Patna. The literacy campaign in Bihar province was so big that it resembled a stampede. Nobody had ever attempted to handle an educational problem as large as this, and it had burst all bounds. It was education run wild!

Mr. Mukherjee took me also to Gaya Prison, where I saw seventeen hundred prisoners studying in classes on the floor of sixty prison buildings, and nearly all the prisoners already literate. I seldom get stage fright, but I didn't know how to act as these prisoners rose from their seats, shouted my name, and burst into terrifically loud singing. The superintendent, Colonel J. Chandra, M. D., had wonderful ideas for prison reform. He had the prison almost wholly self-managing, with a government elected by the prisoners. Very little attention was paid to the gate, Dr. Chandra said, for the prisoners would rather live inside the prison than out! I saw what love and light can do with a prison. Toward the end of that incredible day, the prison cabinet met and their best poet, Syed Abdul Mannan Shayar, sang a song, while I wept with the prisoners who listened. This was the poem, as written down by one of the officials with not a word changed:

The spring season has set in for our souls and the name of God has a new charm and the garden of my heart a fresh beauty. Praise be to God for his grace to the prisoners of our jail, for he has been exceedingly gracious in dealing with us. Oh, kind Lord of goodness, I will sacrifice myself for your sake, for I have discovered what kindness and graciousness really mean. The days of my sighs and groans are over and another voice is in my life.

I was not free inside this jail, nor was I free even before I came; but today there is a new longing in my heart. We Indians have been living in the prison of utter ignorance, but now the good news has reached us that a new day is dawning. No longer shall we be slaves of black ignorance. Who am I that I dare dream such new aspirations as I now cherish? Why should we not entertain our guest in this prison? My prayer is different altogether, O Shayar. Everybody is praying for the happiness of our august guest, but my prayer surpasses all others and exceeds all measure. How fortunate we are that we should have him in our midst as our guest, for he hails from the land of the free! His kindness to us prisoners beggars all description. It is the heart's magnet that has drawn him from far-off America and brought him to us who are in jail. How can the atoms praise and do justice to the sun? Pray convey this humble message of ours to America, that all Indians are full of praise for the Americans. Please tell your countrymen that the unique discoveries of Americans have opened our eyes and that we are only taking a leaf out of your books and faithfully following in your footsteps.

I went home that night limp with emotion, and for most of the night I lay awake in bed, thinking of the vast multitude, nearly three-fifths of all the people in the world, in the prison of ignorance. I knew that they all would stampede toward the light the moment they saw hope, as did the pathetic multitudes I had seen in Bihar.

There was no sleep on the train from Calcutta down to the province of Orissa. The track was so rough one had to hold on to one's bunk and hope that the wheels would also hold on to the rails. They did, and the next day the train arrived intact at the city of Cuttack, the capital. I was taken at once to the office of the Minister of Education in the provincial government, who said, "You shall have the best artists and educators we have and all the money you need. Go ahead."

We set immediately about the arduous task of preparing lessons in the Oriya language with an alphabet I had never set eyes on before. We got on wonderfully, though our artists grumbled at working twelve hours a day. The finished lessons were shown to the Prime Minister, who commended them highly and promised his support in a literacy campaign.

Besides building lessons I spoke to twelve assemblies in five days, one an evening meeting in the open air at which an amplifying system enabled me to reach the vast crowd trailing off into the distant darkness. Furthermore, mission schools, teacher-training schools for men and for women, and colleges all had to be given instructions in between lesson-making hours! The campaign that followed my visit to Orissa has since been "immense," in the words of their director of education.

At the end of that strenuous week I returned to Calcutta, and went from there by train and boat to Biri Siri in Assam, far to the northeast. Here the language with which we worked was called Garo. We began chart building with nationals and Australian and American Baptist missionaries, keen, energetic, and thorough. Our Garo artists were not clever, but they were tireless and determined not to stop until they had done their best. They not only worked on pictures all day but stayed up for two nights practically without sleep. In two days we had finished a set of Garo lessons in Roman letters for the mountain people of Assam and another set in Bengali letters for the lowland people. Similar lessons have since been made by missionaries in six other languages of Assam.

The last night at Biri Siri keeps returning to mind with a strange persistency. A wandering Christian *sadhu*, or religious devotee, had come to the church to sing the story of Christ. As he sang, his eyes were lifted to heaven and his face was transformed like that of an angel. As his high tenor voice floated out over that audience, holding the people in breathless attention, he seemed lost in the bliss of heaven. Though I did not understand his words I was sure I could understand his lovely soul. If Christ does sometimes come back to earth, he was there in the humble Garo church on the edge of Assam that night, for the *sadhu* looked and sounded and acted like a reincarnation of Jesus all during his rapturous singing. I rushed up to him at the close and said to the interpreter, "Tell him I saw Christ in him as he sang. Oh, tell him that, please, in Bengali." The *sadhu* looked at me for a second, then turned away toward the children. He saw Christ in the children but not in me.

Jamshedpur—also called Tatanagar or Tata City—is the home of the gigantic Tata Iron and Steel Works, largest in the British Empire. The whole city is owned and ruled by the company. Here early in March I found a first-rate literacy campaign was already in full swing under a secretary of mass literacy, who showed me twenty adult literacy classes being taught at night. Mr. J. J. Ghandy, general manager of the company, was so interested that he had printed a lengthy address urging every laborer to learn to read.

At Ghaziabad, seven hundred miles to the northwest, near Delhi, in the heart of a huge mass movement, were gathered a hundred delegates, men and women of great earnestness. Though we worked as usual on new lessons in Hindustani, this was no ordinary conference.

They took me to a *mela*—a religious festival—where thousands of Christians, all former outcastes, had gathered from the surrounding region. While we were eating dinner I heard weird music and stole away alone to the large central tent to see what was going on. One of the outcastes was dancing and chanting while hundreds of others swayed and shouted their approval. Feeling grew ever more intense as the frantic dancer gesticulated, his mood swiftly changing from hatred to anguish and grim resolve. Suddenly he seized a boy in front of him, held him aloft a moment, and hurled him to the ground in one violent gesture of desperation. "What is it? What do they mean?" I asked of J. Holmes Smith, a great friend of the outcastes, who had slipped in beside me. "They are depicting the despair of the outcastes in their struggle for emancipation," he explained, "and the triumph of Jesus Christ over untouchability."

After the tense drama, presented with such moving realism, the missionaries conducted a service of Christian worship. We felt the very spirit of Christ to be with us in that tent. A hundred persons received baptism and nearly the entire throng participated in the celebration of the Lord's Supper. Their clothes were still the same, but their hearts were new and their faces shone! Oh, you who despair of Christ's transforming the human race, if only you could see a *mela* in India where the titanic epic of man's transformation into the divinity of sons of God is telescoped into one brief, tense hour! If you could see that, you would never again doubt that Christ is the world's hope!

At Lahore—the capital of the Punjab, a night's journey farther north—my heart went out to a group of fiery students called the "Anti-Illiteracy War Council," who had the Bureau of Education worried sick because they wanted to cut all the red tape and go ahead and make the Punjab literate immediately by geometrical progression! They wanted to cajole, bully, buy, and force all the educated people to teach illiterates or make them pay a fine. They were telling the whole city of Lahore that the Bureau of Education was asleep.

The radical steps these boys wanted were:

1. Fifteen days of intensive propaganda, with handbills, posters, radio broadcasts, leaflets from airplanes, songs about literacy on the streets, processions.

2. A pledge from every literate man either to teach one person each month or to pay a rupee for that month until Lahore was literate.

3. All schools to have vacations of three months, but every student required to teach during school hours every day instead of studying.

The honorable Minister of Education was thoroughly vexed and asked me what I thought could be done to suppress such rash youth. I replied, "It seems to me the safest thing is to give them all the rope they want and then try to keep up with them!"

At the Gakhar Normal School for Moslem Teachers, two hundred Moslem students were being trained to teach adults. Principal Yamini had already caught the idea of our picture-chain lessons and had prepared a good set when I arrived. Only, being a classical scholar, he insisted on using words the illiterates did not understand. In the Punjab the Moslem scholars were convinced that the illiterates ought to learn to read Urdu, the language of culture, or nothing! They were unanimous against teaching the despised Punjabi, which everybody speaks and almost nobody who is anybody reads! Even the professors speak Punjabi among themselves.

The students of the Gakhar Normal School practised on the village of Kot Nura, two miles away. Here before a crowd of a thousand peasants I was asked to give fifty new literates their certificates. Perhaps two hundred others were studying in little classes of five to ten in number. Village classes like these at Kot Nura were springing up in nearly every corner of India.

Swinging far south again and west we found at Rutlam, in Central India, a tremendous mass movement in progress.

Thirty thousand Bhils, an aboriginal people, had been baptized in three years! The nerves of the missionaries from the United Church of Canada were taut to the point of snapping—they were exhausted with success. Now this multitude of illiterate and half-civilized Christians needed to be taught to read and write. "They are one hundred per cent illiterate," I was told, "and there is no literature in their language except some of the Gospels." We asked a pastor how many of his members could read. The pastor said, "I have three thousand members and have taught twenty-six so they can read the Bible."

It was now late March and the thermometer reached 102° every day. In the noon sun a government Packard came one day and carried me a hundred blistering miles to the government guest house at Indore. In ten minutes I was at the bottom of a tub of cool water, and in that tub I stayed until my hosts came to take me to tea.

That night, in spite of the heat, we opened a conference with eight hundred people, many of them in full dress and many in government uniforms. A profuse letter was read from the Premier, containing extravagant adjectives about myself that fitted the facts about as well as a horse collar would have fitted my neck. But I had begun to understand the psychology of India and made no effort to correct exaggerations. The leaders of India had made up their minds to launch an onslaught on illiteracy, and they needed a figure-head from some distant land to give the signal—somebody about whom they knew nothing and who thus made it possible for them to give limitless range to their imaginations. I had succeeded somewhere, which was all that mattered. The one thing India needed above all else was faith to believe it could be done. So the Indore Literacy Campaign was launched that night with a blare of trumpets.

The next morning six hundred Indore teachers gathered for instructions; as though they could receive a course in two hours! I gave them two hours' worth of faith that India can be literate and a few principles of the psychology of teaching an illiterate: "Never scold nor frown nor yawn; say 'yes' when you mean 'no'; look surprised and pleased and pat the student on the back and tell him how bright he is; tell him he will make a wonderful teacher and that you want him to help you teach the rest of the village; treat him like a rajah, and make him like you; don't say a single unnecessary word, but let the student talk all he will; never ask a question the illiterate cannot answer; never tell him what he already knows."

This psychology of teaching—all of it directly contrary to Indian custom, where they believe the old maxim, "Spare the rod and spoil the child"—is about fifty per cent of the art of teaching illiterates. It sounded like an educational revolution to the teachers of India. They thought being so kind might work with adults if you taught only one at a time—but with children, God forbid!

In this vast central and western region of India with its many native states is Daly College for the training of princes, which I was invited to visit. Every one of the sixty princes wore a sky-blue turban. They had smooth handsome faces and great black eyes, just like the princes of the story books. I had a queer sensation of unreality while talking to them. They all promised to do their part to make their states literate, but they did not have a passion for the poor in their eyes, and I wondered whether any of my words would really sink in. I got not half the sense of irresistible power that came as I talked to Isabella Thoburn College, for example, or the wonderful educational committee of the Indian National Congress.

As I rolled into the station at Baroda the next morning at one forty-five I was met by four Hindu students and a Christian missionary. They said they had come to invite me to the literacy conference they were holding that afternoon in an Indian school. Then to my amazement the students tossed a garland of jasmine about my neck. How can one help loving people who meet you at 1:45 A.M. with invitations and jasmine!

It was Sunday morning when I reached Ahmedabad, the great industrial city north of Bombay, and spoke to a thousand Christians at eight o'clock in a united service arranged by several churches and missions. I told them that since so many people in India lacked the Christian passion to teach without pay, each Christian ought to teach four to make up for the slackers who would not teach at all. When I asked how many in that audience would volunteer, they all stood up.

At the service for all religions that evening I told them that that morning a thousand Christians had each promised to teach four others. Six hundred more rose to promise that they would each teach at least two illiterates during that year. Even though most of them were not Christians, I think they would have promised four instead of two, if they had been asked. I felt there, as I did many times in India, that the great yearning love of the missionaries was doing more to rebuild the spiritual and educational life of India than any other single factor. The Reverend G. N. Brown, my amazingly competent host, had advertised so well that he gathered one huge crowd after another.

On Monday morning at eight o'clock, six hundred Hindus, Moslems, Jains, and Christians gathered in a public hall. That afternoon they were there again. The next morning at eight there were seven hundred present, that afternoon six hundred, that evening a thousand! The same six hundred people had returned for five meetings to hear more and more and more, and still more. Fortunately, by this time I had accumulated enough convictions to make five speeches on literacy without repeating. I took the night train, tired but happy—and slept!

As the train pulled into Kosamba early Thursday morning, I was strapping my bedding in leisurely fashion when I heard the sound of Scottish bagpipes. I looked out the window to find a band of pipers in full Scottish outfit, bright plaid kilts and impudent Scottish hats—nothing was missing except the glowing pink complexions of real Scots. For these pipers were young Indians, and behind them as far as my eye could reach was a throng of people. The whole town was out to meet the train. What celebrity,

I wondered, was arriving? Was it Gandhi, or the Viceroy, or perhaps the Gaekwar of Baroda himself?

My question was soon answered. In a moment a company of town officials filed into the train and approached me. "Is Gandhi here, or the Gaekwar?" I asked their leader, who proved to be Dr. R. D. Souri, representing His Excellency the Premier. "No," answered Dr. Souri, "we have gathered here to meet you and to receive you as a state guest of the government of Baroda." Then, following the recognized Indian custom of presenting an address of welcome on such occasions, he began to read:

"Our government as a mark of recognition to the services rendered by you for the whole country of India have commanded me to welcome you as a guest of his Highness' government on this March 30, 1939, at Kosamba, where you have so kindly agreed to lead a joint conference of the state government teachers, inspecting officers, missionaries, and their education staff. . . ."

I was completely overcome by the honor and the fulsome praise contained in the rest of the address, but I smiled benignly and tried to look like a distinguished visitor! So we started from the station, the bagpipers leading, and behind us the school children of thirty-five schools, which had been dismissed for the occasion. As we reached the huge open space that had been decorated for the ceremonies, what struck my eye first was the side of a large building on which had been painted the words of the song that we had prepared as one means of teaching the phonetics. It is sung fast and loud:

Everybody's singing ka, ke, ki, ko, ku
All the boys are singing ka, ke, ki, ko, ku
All the girls are singing ka, ke, ki, ko ku
All Baroda's singing ka, ke, ki, ko, ku.

We stopped in front of the building and four thousand school children sang that song until people must have heard it in Mars. Then there was a celebration for the entire town—food for everybody. People of all castes ate together. Dr. Souri was thrilled to tell me that outcastes were waiting on us, and even some of the caste people were unafraid of contamination. It doesn't matter about Christians, for we are outcastes, too. Christians are a queer sort of outcastes, cast out *above* rather than *below,* in the estimation of other Indians. One doesn't mind being an outcaste if he is cast "up and out" instead of "down and out."

Before that whole throng one of the women missionaries, Miss Laura Austin, taught an illiterate man to read in Gujerati, easily and swiftly. When he saw how utterly easy it was to learn, his face lighted up with a triumphant happiness. Mr. S. V. Mukerjee, Revenue Commissioner, then spoke with trembling voice as he said, "Today we are beholding a miracle. It is written on that new literate's face."

They had one special feature after another all day— and in between each, the Scottish bagpipers! It was, they kept telling me, the dawn of a new era for Baroda. Happiness began to beam on faces that looked as though they had never used their smile muscles before. I felt here, as I had in Gaya jail and at the Christian *mela* of former outcastes at Ghaziabad, the rising of something enormous —as though the figure of Hope, blindfolded and playing on the one unbroken string of her harp, were about to have the blindfold removed. This huge celebration symbolized for those masses of people the hope of their emancipation from ignorance.

And yet I was afraid of the thing I was doing in India— unloosing something that had been chained since the dawn of time. Nearly three-fifths of the human race might in a few years be throbbing with a new, nameless, terrible hope as were these people. If Christian missions can lead this new uprising, if the way can be opened for Christ to satisfy the hunger of these new literates, they will be the meek who will inherit and bless the earth. But if, after starting this thing, we allow the leadership to slip from the Christian brotherhood in all lands, if this unthinkably vast multitude become educated with pagan ideals, God pity the future.

> O masters, lords and rulers of all lands,
> How will the Future reckon with this Man?
> How answer his brute questions in that hour
> When whirlwinds of rebellion shake the world?
> How will it be with kingdoms and with kings—
> With those who shaped him to the thing he is—
> When this dumb Terror shall reply to God
> After the silence of the centuries?[1]

[1] From *The Man With the Hoe and Other Poems*, by Edwin Markham. Used by permission of Virgil Markham.

I went to sleep on the train repeating with Edwin Markham, "after the silence of the centuries"—and awoke in Bombay. It was just five days until the official opening of what was to be India's most tremendous literacy campaign, in Marathi, Gujerati, and Urdu, headed by the Prime Minister of Bombay Presidency. Bombay with a million illiterates! They were to hold their inaugural meeting on April 4. That day they would begin to propagandize the entire city, using motion pictures, posters, slogans, processions, public meetings, and handbills from airplanes. They asked the city to contribute 400,000 rupees and they wanted two thousand volunteers for their five hundred classrooms. My good friend, Mr. S. R. Bhagwat, mayor of Poona, was beaming. This was the kind of war he had wanted for years. Never before had I felt so reluctant to leave anywhere as I did that day when I had to leave Bombay before the campaign actually opened.

But another exciting program had been set up for me at Sangli, in the southern part of the province. Mayor Bhagwat went with me. Officials of Sangli State, missionaries, pastors, and many other delegates had collected from that area.

At the home of Dr. J. L. Goheen, of the American Presbyterian mission, we set to work revising the Marathi lessons and making a large picture-chain chart. We finished that particular revision in one day. It was 104° in the shade, but we forgot the heat in our excitement, for here was the kind of committee one dreams about. In addition to lesson-making, we held eleven public sessions on literacy with from one hundred to three hundred persons in attendance at each. On leaving we were entertained at tea in the royal gardens of Sangli State by the Maharajah and his lovely Maharani.

There was just time before sailing from Colombo to make a flying trip to Nagpur for a meeting of the budget committee of the National Christian Council. "If we had a million dollars," I told them, "your organization could lead India to literacy." They appointed Miss Ruth Ure, of the Presbyterian mission in the Punjab, to travel throughout India as the leader of the literacy cause, but all they are able to find for her is twenty-five hundred dollars yearly with which to work. A few thousand! How pitifully small these funds are in view of the opportunities all around us!

The second World War prevented my returning to India and Africa in 1940, but the mighty campaigns that began in 1939 are continuing. In every state and province of India, provincial governments, city governments, and missions are working hand in hand. A hundred million in India have been stirred with a new longing that India never knew before—the longing to learn to read and write. Millions have already learned, but this is only the beginning, and India is desperately in need of America's help for the completion of this titanic task.

CHAPTER EIGHT

Literacy and a Good Neighbor Policy

THE experiences described in the preceding chapters have made me an optimist in the face of our present tragedy. I have seen how easy it is to win the friendship of people—people anywhere—if only we approach them in a spirit of unselfish sharing. The world is divided into an infinity of small groups, each expecting hostility from the other and therefore on the defensive. There is suspicion between white and colored races, between religions, between nationals and "foreigners," between rich and poor, capital and labor, between educated and illiterate, between those speaking different languages, between families and often within families. When we seek to serve groups outside our own, we must prove our friendship and patiently wait for this initial suspicion to disappear, and this requires self-control, for one's instinct is to give like for like, snub for snub, dislike for dislike.

But self-restraint and tact can replace this defense mechanism with mutual good will. It has been thrilling to discover how quickly such ventures as literacy campaigns, disease control, and agricultural missions melt away these dislikes and suspicions. The glad good news I want to shout from the housetops is that America can work a world miracle, if we care enough and serve selflessly enough—that it is far, far easier than we ever could have dreamed.

It is not only easy but it is enormously important. For we now seem to be emerging into a new age, when instead of many little antagonistic worlds we hope to have world brotherhood and a world government. It is a glorious hope, but it will come only as people of different cultures and backgrounds learn kindly toleration and glory in "united diversity." While statesmen feel their way to political world union, we must find great enterprises like the common struggle against illiteracy to bring about confidence and the will to cooperate without which political union will be impossible.

Everything that is happening today is pushing America more irrevocably, whether she will or not, out into every corner of the world. When the smoke of this war clears away we will not again draw back in our shell like a snail—not this time! Our youth will pour into ten thousand communities all over this planet to teach and to serve, just as our teachers have gone to the Philippines during these past twenty years and our missionaries have gone to foreign lands. America's influence will be felt to the corners of the earth.

The second World War, with its incredible development

of air transportation, has shattered American isolationism. Planes that can cross the oceans and return without refueling have thrown every country into our back yard. Turn a radio dial and listen to Chungking, Cairo, Moscow, Sydney. "Who is my neighbor?" Every man, every race, and every country! No nation is any longer safe until the whole world is safe. We cannot have peace anywhere until there is peace everywhere. Isolation is out.

But now America faces the immensely fateful question: "Just how are we going to wield our influence to make a better world?" We hear two directly opposite proposals. One man says, "Continue to police the world, we and Great Britain. Put the fear of God into anybody who does not go with us. Have a navy bigger than all the rest of the world combined. Don't let any other countries have airplanes. Rule the air, the waves, and the land." But another voice replies, "If we try to police the world while we and Britain enjoy better economic conditions than the rest, they will hate us, and ultimately bring about our downfall. The only stable and just peace will come if we serve the other nations and invite them to join us in building a cooperative world." This second way is the Christian and the democratic way; but will it work? Fortunately, we have had some experiences that prove that it will work and that the cost is trivial as compared to the maintenance of armies and navies.

Look, for example, at the experience of the United States in the Philippines. In spite of our determination to "mind our own business" and stay away from the Eastern

Hemisphere, we became responsible for those islands quite against our desires. We were at war with Spain; a Spanish fleet was in Manila Bay. Dewey sank the fleet, and the Philippines were on our hands. We would have dropped them if we could, but since that seemed out of the question we decided in a fever of idealism to do the best we could with them. We made mistakes in our administration, to be sure, but we may be immeasurably proud of one fact, that we made the welfare of the people objective number one and not exploitation; proud because it is the first and only time in history that a dominant power gave more consideration to educating the people than to exploiting them. We sent thousands of American teachers to the Philippines, and they raised the literacy of the Philippines from something like five per cent to seventy-five per cent—in forty-four years! Their Malay neighbors in the Dutch East Indies, the same race of people, are still only five per cent literate after three hundred years of Dutch rule; these are the official Dutch figures. No wonder President Quezon and Carlos Romulo, Vice-President of International Rotary, never tire of praising America because we "were there to educate the people and not to exploit them."

Then we granted them freedom, to become operative in 1946. That is why their loyalty and gratitude have amazed the world, while all the other dependent peoples in Asia have betrayed their overlords. America proved in the Philippines that it pays to be a good neighbor.

A few years ago nearly all the Latin American countries hated and feared the United States. President Herbert

	ala	escalera	iglesia	ojo	uña
ala	a	e	i	o	u
martillo	ma	me	mi	mo	mu
naranja	na	ne	ni	no	nu
dado	da	de	di	do	du
zapato	za	ze	zi	zo	zu
palma	pa	pe	pi	po	pu
tambor	ta	te	ti	to	tu
sandía	sa	se	si	so	su
bandera	ba	be	bi	bo	bu
jaula	ja	je	ji	jo	ju
vaca	va	ve	vi	vo	vu
hacha	ha	he	hi	ho	hu
ratón	ra	re	ri	ro	ru
gato	ga	ge	gi	go	gu
farol	fa	fe	fi	fo	fu
lápiz	la	le	li	lo	lu
caballo	ca	que	qui	co	cu

SPANISH PICTURE-CHAIN CHART

Hoover started a Good Neighbor program, which President Roosevelt has continued. The result is that today nearly every Latin American country is our friend. Latin America proves that we can win the friendship of other nations, if we try hard enough.

China is another wonderful illustration of the power of loving service. The vast majority of Americans do not realize how much missionaries had to do with making China our friend. For three centuries the Chinese had been mortally afraid that Europe would tear their land to pieces—as Europe actually did divide Africa and southern Asia among its powers. So much did the Chinese fear Europe that a hundred years ago no white man was permitted in any part of their country except where white soldiers forced open the doors. The Chinese government would execute any one of its citizens who was caught teaching his language to a foreigner or translating any foreign book into Chinese.

Robert Morrison, the first Protestant missionary, had to work in secret while translating the Bible into Mandarin. But other missionaries kept coming, dozens, hundreds, thousands, and each of them was building a little island of friendship. Christian Chinese caught Christ's vision of human brotherhood and his plan of joining hands in love around the world to build the kingdom of heaven on earth. So China for a century was swinging like a pendulum between fear of foreign imperialism on the one hand, and love of the missionaries on the other.

In 1900 came the Boxer Uprising to wipe out all white

foreigners. Europe and the United States put down that uprising, and an indemnity was demanded. Historians say it was ten times as high as the damage China had done to foreign property—three hundred and twenty-five millions. American missionaries persuaded the United States to return our share of the indemnity, seventeen million dollars, to be used for scholarships for Chinese students. Some of the students who benefited by that money now rule China. That is why China is America's friend.

The President of China, Generalissimo Chiang Kai-shek, and his wife are Christians. The majority of the present cabinet are Christians. In normal times more Bibles are distributed in China than in any other foreign country. Dr. Hu Shih, the great Chinese philosopher, when Ambassador to the United States said at a China Relief dinner in New York, "I am not a Christian, but I love the missionaries, and every Chinese loves them, for they did not run when the Japanese invaded our country, but risked their lives for us."

When you and I review the fruitage of the good neighbor idea in the Philippines, China, and Latin America, it becomes clear that we have the power to create an era of good will in the whole world if we go after it—if we can be unselfish and big-hearted enough—if we really love. Not only can we do it; we must do it. If we fail, this world will plunge into a hell worse than that of the second World War.

Titanic Asia, with more than half of the world's population, is awake and determined to catch up with the West.

She hesitates between two voices. Christians talk to her of the Christ vision, ask her to join hands around the world, forgetting race and color, to build a paradise— "Thy Kingdom come, thy will be done on earth." "We have enough science and mechanical genius and raw materials," they say. "All we need is loving cooperation." On the other hand, the voices of hatred and prejudice are working to persuade Asia to gang up against the white race. If the voice of love wins, Asia will become the world's great new blessing. If the voice of racial hatred wins, Asia will become the world's great curse. As goes Asia, so goes this planet.

There is terrible danger that after this war is over a weakened white race may find itself in deadly conflict with the colored races. If Asia should unite against the whites, Africa would be with her—together they would have four hundred millions more than all the whites in the world. The end of such a combination would be enslavement of the white race. Many of our leaders believe we are headed for that right now.

But it is wholly useless, for it is amazingly easy to win the friendship of the peoples of Asia and Africa, if we will be Christlike enough to serve and love them unselfishly. The race problem is not a colored problem, it is a white problem.

So America confronts a truly awful decision. She cannot escape making an answer. Shall she help the world rise toward heaven or allow it to rush down toward a hell worse than it has ever known? America holds the fate of the world balanced in her hand, and her own fate as well.

We must begin an all-out good neighbor program for the whole world such as we have been promoting in the Western Hemisphere, a program in which government and churches will work as we did in the Philippines to prove our love by our service.

One of the chief channels now wide open through which we may prove our love is to help countries that are struggling with illiteracy. It is far more than "a nice thing to do"; it is a realistic project in building world good will.

The "each one teach one" literacy program has special merit in generating good will. We are not only serving the world, but we are persuading them to help each other—spreading the idea of service without pay. We are creating the atmosphere in which other countries will be able to cooperate with us and with one another. The longer I do this work of persuading people to stop being selfish and help others, the more clearly I see that the greatest stumbling block to progress is the ugly habit of doing nothing unless "it pays." "Service for profit" is not saving the world. In these literacy campaigns we are fostering the ideal that churches always preach, the one indispensable cohesive force without which there can be no united world—unselfish love in action. Our "each one teach one" ideal is the central truth in the social teachings of Christ: love thy neighbor as thyself, and do unto others as you would have others do unto you. We have not only "answered right" in these campaigns, but we have put love into action.

It goes even deeper than that. The world is cursed by cleavages that prevent cooperation, and no gulf is deeper than that between the educated and the ignorant masses. The "each one teach one" method bridges that gulf. The higher classes become proud of their startlingly democratic behavior. The Prince of Aundh sits down beside an illiterate and teaches him to read. A former Brahman puts his arm around an untouchable while he teaches him. It is just such projects as these multiplied all over the earth in a million villages and towns that will break down class walls so that we can build a new world.

Another deep chasm in many countries is that between religions and sects. The cause of literacy furnishes one of the finest common tasks in which people of different faiths will work shoulder to shoulder. This book has many concrete instances showing how Hindus, Buddhists, Moslems, and Christians are teaching illiterates in loving cooperation; for the spirit of mutual helpfulness that underlies the "each one teach one" program tends to draw all men's hearts together, so that they forget their differences and think instead of their common aspirations.

I covet for all Christian workers everywhere the opportunity to serve the cause of literacy. There are places where missionaries, especially those with separatist inclinations, have allowed themselves to be pushed off into little eddies wholly outside the main stream of the life around them, leaving them unhappy and almost devoid of influence. Such missionaries really misrepresent Jesus, who horrified the Pharisees because he talked and ate with "publicans and sinners." I have seen literacy campaigns pull many churches and missions into the very mainstream of public life, making them more gloriously useful than ever before.

I have seen discouraged missionaries filled with new hope and new power as they went about teaching illiterates and persuading whole communities to engage in the same loving service. They discovered that the spirit of Christ was not only good for individuals but that it became a catalytic agent, to borrow a useful term from chemistry, in the presence of which literates would love and teach illiterates. Governments launching literacy campaigns are finding the spirit of missionaries and Christian workers indispensable to create this zest for humble service, in which people will teach the lowest classes without being paid. So the officials look on the missionaries in a new light, as people who have the spirit without which the country cannot become educated. People begin to tell one another that the progress of their country depends upon their catching the love of Christ. When they see this, they have discovered the highest truth this world has to learn —that the one thing we still need in order to insure marvelous progress is for men to become Christlike enough to serve others without profit for themselves.

Or if we consider the permanence of the church in mission lands, literacy is of immeasurable importance. We expect those young churches to survive for centuries—and they may be very stormy centuries. Dr. Eric North in *The Book of a Thousand Tongues* shows that in the past only those churches that had the Bible in their own tongue have survived persecution:

The sections of the Eastern Church—Greek, Armenian, Georgian, Syrian, Coptic, and Ethiopic—from the beginning had the Scriptures in the vernaculars of their adherents, and these churches have survived the storms to which they have been subjected through the centuries. On the other hand, the great churches founded in North Africa from Rome had the Bible in Latin only, a foreign tongue which effectively closed the Book to the common people. When the waves of Islam swept along the southern littoral of the Mediterranean, these churches could not survive the storm and they perished.

The same truth has been demonstrated on the mission field. The church had flourishing missions in China, Korea, and Japan in the fourteenth and fifteenth centuries, but they failed to give their converts the Bible in their mother tongue, and when persecution came, their churches were practically wiped out of existence.[1]

Dr. North cites a particularly telling illustration in Madagascar, where no amount of persecution was able to stamp out the faith of Christians. In the early nineteenth century the missionaries first came to that island. By 1835 eighteen thousand copies of the New Testament, Psalms, and other parts of the Bible had been distributed in the native tongue, and about two hundred persons had become

[1] From *The Bible among Men*, by J. H. Ritson, quoted in *The Book of a Thousand Tongues*, edited by Eric M. North, pp. 13-14. New York, Harper & Brothers, 1938.

Christians. But the pagan queen of Madagascar set up a fierce persecution, forbade Christian worship, and drove the missionaries out of the country. The native Christians were tortured, executed, burned at the stake. The faithful kept the Scriptures hidden in caves, or buried in the ground, read them at night, memorized them, and passed them secretly from one to another. For twenty-five years that persecution went on, and ten thousand people were estimated to have suffered. At the end of that period there were thousands of Christians. At the beginning there had been only two hundred! A Bible-reading church thrives on persecution.

One fact, then, is clear: where young churches are growing, their members must be able to read. The Bible has been translated in part or in whole into ten hundred and fifty-five languages for probably ninety-five per cent of the world's population. Wonderful! But only forty per cent of the world's population is literate. Among non-Christians not even fifteen per cent are able to read; for the other eighty-five the Bible is a closed book, and the only way to open the book is to open their illiterate eyes.

Teaching people to read, therefore, is not only important—it is indispensable, and the census figures show us that it has been the weakest spot in our entire mission program. Some missionaries thought they ought to "stick to the gospel" and let the government educate illiterates. Others thought it was a waste of their university training to sit down by the hour beside illiterates and teach ABC's, and so they devoted their time to teaching leaders or reaching the *literati*. Others gave their high talents to translating and writing. And so teaching illiterates, the humblest and easiest and neediest of tasks, was neglected just because it was too simple and elementary for highly trained men and women. All this is now rapidly changing, for missionaries everywhere are becoming aware that teaching people to read is as essential for the permanence and growth of the church as translating the Bible or preaching the gospel. Nowhere is this new point of view developing more rapidly than in the Roman Catholic church.

Thus no matter how we look at literacy, whether from the point of view of building a better world or of building a permanent church, the challenge for American Christians is immense beyond imagination. It makes my blood tingle! Even in the midst of the black days through which we are now passing, I am an incurable optimist. I have seen how easy it is to win the hearts of the world's underprivileged and forgotten masses, how inexpensive, how delightful, how permanent. I know from experience that "love never faileth"!

But this task is going to require more love than American Christians have heretofore expressed in their world enterprises. We must rise to the measure of self-sacrifice that the Quakers have shown and learn to give more than the crumbs that fall from our tables. It would be a terrifying exposure of our true natures if we could give our billions and our sons to defeat our enemies and could not give even an infinitesimal fraction of what the present war is costing to build the good will to prevent this madness from sweeping the world again. The same sacrificial spirit that millions are manifesting in this war must be carried over into the peace. Some of us must give ourselves and our children. Some must give our dollars, some will give millions, and all of us must pour into the cause that mighty, mysterious, magnetic force of prayer, which multiplies every dollar and every man's effort a thousandfold.

We ought right now to be building up a fund for the cause of literacy—a million dollars for Africa, another million for South America, and two millions for Asia—so that we can start helping these countries immediately the war is over.

Christians across America, as I have told them about literacy, have exclaimed hundreds of times, "This is the most stupendous challenge in the whole world!" It is indeed one of the finest openings ever given the church through which she may bless the whole human race and pour the love of Christ into human society. It is God's awful call to Christians in this awful hour.

America, you have the chance of ten thousand years to help the world! Our peace and world peace demand that we shall grow large enough and become Christlike soon enough to lavish our love in humble service for the whole world. If we use this rich opportunity to carry Christ to Asia and Africa, then peace-loving China with a fourth of the world's population, peace-loving India with one-fifth of all the people in the world, and the meek, song-loving Africans will join us in building "a kingdom of heaven on earth." Then at last "the meek shall inherit the earth."

Index